An Unexpected Journal

CELEBRATING PLANET NARNIA

10 YEARS IN ORBIT

ADVENT 2018
VOLUME 1, ISSUE 4

Copyright © 2018 - An Unexpected Journal.
Print Edition

MANAGING EDITOR: Zak Schmoll
JOURNAL MARK: Erika McMillan
LAYOUT & DESIGN BY: Marshall Arthur Liszt

EDITORS:

Carla Alvarez	Sandra Hicks	Daniel Ray
Elizabeth Connor	Lucas W. Holt	Zak Schmoll
Annie Crawford	Nicole Howe	Daniel Semelsberger
John Creech	Korine Martinez	Jason Smith
Virginia de la Lastra	Erica McMillan	Edward Stengel
Alison DeLong	Jason Monroe	Charlotte Thomason
Karise Gililland	Seth Myers	Rebekah Valerius
Ryan Grube	Annie Nardone	Hannah Zarr
Jamie Hay	Josiah Peterson	

CONTRIBUTORS:

Adam L. Brackin	Virginia de la Lastra	John Mark Reynolds
Annie Crawford	Louis Markos	Lancia E. Smith
Brenton Dickieson	Jason Monroe	Michael Ward
Ryan Grube	Holly Ordway	Donald T. Williams
Malcolm Guite	Josiah Peterson	Kyoko Yuasa

All rights reserved. This book is protected by the copyright laws of the United States of America. No part of this publication may be reproduced, distributed or transmitted in any form or by any means, or stored in a database or retrieval system, without the prior written permission of the publisher.

An Unexpected Journal
Houston, TX
http://anunexpectedjournal.com
anunexpectedjournal@gmail.com

Contents

The Wood Between the Worlds • V. de la Lastra 4
For Your Contemplation • Ryan Grube 5
Warm Cup / Conversation • Lancia E. Smith 8
Seven Questions • AUJ with Michael Ward 9
Ward/Robe • Lancia E. Smith 23
Where Paradoxes Play • J. Perez 24
Why We Love to Visit Narnia • L. Markos 31
A Unexpected Journey • J.M. Reynolds 39
A Seven-Days' Journey through the Heavens • H. Ordway ...46
Ward / Guite • Lancia E. Smith 48
Planet Narnia As Creative Inspiration • M. Guite 49
The Daily Planet • M. Guite 52
Circle Dance • M. Guite 54
C.S. Lewis: A Life • D.T. Williams 56
(Re)Considering the Planet Narnia Thesis • B. Dickieson 59
A Defense of Planet Narnia • J. Peterson 79
Return to Planet Narnia • M. Ward 90
Table Narnia • K. Yuasa 109
The Cure Has Begun • A. Crawford 127
VDT & The Rehabilitation of Practical Reason • J. Monroe ..139
Gravitational Pull • Marshall Arthur Liszt 153
Quarantine • A.L. Brackin 155
Bibliography 158
Contributors 163
About 170

The Wood Between the Worlds, Virginia de la Lastra

For Your Contemplation:
What You'll See When You Read This Issue

Ryan Grube

Before 2008, many of us had read C.S. Lewis's works, including his fiction, his apologetics, his works of literary criticism, and even his personal letters. Yet none of us made the connection that now seems obvious. Jupiter, Mars, the Sun, and the rest of the wandering stars had for decades silently exerted their influence upon us while we read *The Chronicles of Narnia*. Our imaginations had been surreptitiously furnished with a Christological inventory Lewis culled from medieval archetypes. Visually speaking, this was all happening in our 'blind spot', along the periphery of our awareness, in the 'enjoyment consciousness', as we now know to call it. Every piece of the puzzle lay hiding in plain sight, waiting for someone to approach Lewis's oeuvre syntopically, perceive the connections, and then share the interpretive key to Narnia.

It has now been ten years since Michael Ward accomplished this with *Planet Narnia*, and the team at AUJ wants to take this opportunity to celebrate the anniversary of publication as well as to convey a measure of appreciation to the man whose epiphanic detective work has done so much to influence academics, theologians, artists, and apologists alike — not to mention the genesis of AUJ itself!

Those who follow the liturgical calendar will notice that this celebratory edition is being issued during Advent. It is indeed a happy coincidence, because this is a time of year when Christians think often of the heavens and their starry host and enjoy the tingle of anticipation that builds each Sunday until Christmas. Such anticipation serves a dual role for us. *Advent* (deriving from Latin) means "to come" or "to arrive". For Christians, this refers to both Christ's incarnation some 2,000 years ago and also his second coming at the close of the age. Each of these two events must be juxtaposed in order for their historical importance and their spiritual implications to become clear, much like the way a stereoscope presents us with a three-dimensional impression of two-dimensional photos.

Similarly, a proper celebration of *Planet Narnia* ought to reflect the multiple dimensions that have been impacted by Ward and his work, yet since our medium (both print and online) is two-dimensional, you will have to consider the contributions to Issue #4 both as individual parts *and* in conjunction with the whole to derive the total meaning and draw out further implications.

To put it simply, juxtapose poets and scholars, photographers and illustrators. See how together they comprise "something made" as well as "something said" (because all too often we look only for the latter and forget to seek out the former). C.S. Lewis put together dwarfs and dryads and unicorns, Father Christmas and Dufflepuds and E. Nesbit-like characters, and those who weren't considering the *poiema* missed the point and passed it off as pastiche. However, Michael Ward noticed this and looked for a deeper harmony, and when he found it he shared it with us, and ten years on we are all better off because he did.

Read on and you will find in these pages an intentional pastiche of works to enjoy: encomiums, arguments, and further evidences; photos, illustrations, and iconic imagery; an interview, a backstory, and an evangel; and also poetry, essays, and even a short-story.

… It all serves to evoke an atmosphere that is both offworldly and Otherworldly at the same time.

Feel free to look for clues if you wish to imitate Michael Ward (imitation being the sincerest form of flattery) in seeking to discover insights and underlying connections. Though nowhere near as monumental as what he found concealed in *The Chronicles*, there is much that lies hidden beneath the surface of Issue #4.

Warm Cup / Conversation
Image © Lancia E. Smith

"If 'Warm Cup / Conversation' is of Spud at the Kilns - that took place Sunday November 24, 2013. The C.S. Lewis Foundation hosted a celebratory tea at The Kilns as a gathering place after the milestone event of Lewis being given a place in Poets' Corner in Westminster Abbey."

- Lancia E Smith

Seven Questions

An Interview with Michael Ward

Michael Ward with AUJ

1. Since Planet Narnia *was first published, you have spent a full decade crossing the globe to deliver lectures, lead workshops, and teach classes about your discovery of Lewis's 'secret'. How has this experience affected you, in terms of your life's trajectory, your academic interests, and your spiritual awareness?*

In terms of 'trajectory' it has opened up all sorts of speaking opportunities that might not otherwise have come my way. In terms of academic interests, it has validated and consolidated my focus on theological imagination. As far as spiritual awareness goes, it has continually reminded me of the importance of 'Enjoyment' in the spiritual life, as distinct from 'Contemplation' — the need to develop one's *connaître* knowledge of God, not just *savoir* knowledge.

More generally, I think a chief effect it has had is to make me more aware of the reach of Lewis's legacy — or we might even say, ministry. He has impacted so many people (young, old, simple, educated, Christian, non-Christian), in so many places (I've spoken to date in about a dozen different countries and in nearly forty of the fifty U.S. States), and at so many levels (intellectual, imaginative, spiritual). It's a great privilege to 'travel in his wake', as it were, to have an opportunity to follow in the aftermath of his influence with the (far smaller and less diverse) gifts that I have myself been given. So I feel I have a responsibility to honour and extend Lewis's legacy in that regard.

I also feel a responsibility to *Planet Narnia* itself, if that doesn't sound like a strange thing to say. But I say it because of something the Inklings scholar, Diana Glyer, once remarked to me about her own (excellent) book, *The Company They Keep: C.S. Lewis and J.R.R. Tolkien as Writers in Community*. It's not enough just to write a book and get it published, any more than it would be enough just to conceive a child and give birth to it. You then have a responsibility to give your work 'a good start' in the world (by giving talks, recording interviews and podcasts, signing copies, responding to readers), and to do what you can to tend its mid-term development in appropriate ways. In my case, that has involved the writing of the shorter, simpler version, *The Narnia Code*, and presenting the BBC documentary of the same title. You get to shepherd your own work for a while, which hopefully increases the chance it will gain a wide and fair hearing and accordingly be able to stand more and more on its own feet. So that has taught me a lot about the job of being a writer; it involves much more than just writing! Of course, the long-term future of anything you produce is not in your hands. At some point, you have to let go and see whether the book sinks or swims. And then you just hope and pray that whatever's good in your work will survive and thrive, even though it's now no longer under your direct parental care.

2. *How have you seen Planet Narnia affect C.S. Lewis studies?*

I've been pleased to see in recent years what I think is a greater appreciation among Lewis readers and scholars of the subtlety and sophistication of his imaginative work and of the unity and coherence of his output. His academic expertise is now seen as much more fully relevant to his creative writing and apologetics than hitherto. I dare to suppose that my work has played a part in that development because I made a deliberate attempt to canvass the whole of his output in *Planet Narnia* — not treating him as merely an 'apologist' or 'fiction writer' or 'medievalist', as many students of Lewis before me had tended to do, but as all three together, and other things besides (e.g. as a poet, and simply as a man, a biographical subject). With regard to treating him as simply 'a man', I was greatly assisted by the publication of the collected letters — the three volumes of which came out between 2000 and 2006. I, like everyone else with an interest in Lewis, owe a huge debt to Walter Hooper in that respect. The increasingly holistic approach to Lewis in scholarship is much more due to Hooper's work than to mine.

Speaking more personally, I think the fact that *Planet Narnia* was published by Oxford University Press and did well, both critically and commercially, meant that Cambridge University Press were more interested in a 'Cambridge Companion' about Lewis than they might otherwise have been. Indeed, CUP told me and my eventual co-editor, Robert MacSwain, that they had turned down two or three previous proposals for such a Companion. Now, the reason they accepted our proposal had a lot to do with its breadth of scope and the distinguished names we got on-board (for which Rob MacSwain deserves much of the credit), but I think the success of *Planet Narnia* also made it easier for CUP to feel confident that Rob and I would do a fair job. And the publication of *The Cambridge Companion to C.S. Lewis*, though not representing any kind of sea-change in Lewis studies, was nonetheless a significant milestone, a sign that it was an increasingly 'respectable' line of intellectual enquiry. At least Rowan Williams suggests that that is the case (see *The Lion's World*, x). And I think that has had a knock-on effect with the upcoming generation of scholars. At any rate, I'm now supervising a couple of Lewis-focused doctorates within the Theology Faculty at Oxford[1] — and they are the first two such doctoral studies ever to be undertaken at his old university. There had been one doctorate on Lewis in the English Faculty at Oxford (completed by Andrew Cuneo in the late 1990s), but these are the first in Theology.

3. What has been the biggest misconception or roadblock you have encountered from your audience while expounding the Planet Narnia *thesis?*

Probably the biggest, or most frequently encountered, misconception is that my thesis is somehow controverted or at least challenged by the fact that Lewis did not have the whole seven-part series mapped out in advance. One person described this as "a massive problem," which surprised me because it doesn't strike me as a problem at all, and indeed I thought I had sufficiently addressed this issue within the pages of *Planet Narnia*.[2] The planetary scheme for the series grew incrementally, starting with Jupiter because Jupiter was his favourite planet, the one he said he himself had been born

---

[1] One of Dr. Ward's doctoral students has also contributed an article to this issue: cf. Jahdiel Perez's piece

[2] Michael Ward, *Planet Narnia* (Oxford: Oxford University Press, 2008), 5, 222.

under, and the one he seemed to regard as especially in need of imaginative rehabilitation in the all-too-Saturnine twentieth century. Then he decided to do a second; then a third; and so on. It was a cumulative project.

Another blockage that I've noticed some people have is with the notion that I have 'cherry-picked' my examples, selecting those pieces of evidence that support the thesis while ignoring those which might subvert it. Again, I felt I had given enough of a defence on that point, when discussing "the insulating power of context."[3] "iconographical ambiguity,"[4] polyvalence,[5] and the fact that "in a certain conjunction of the planets each may play the other's part."[6] But I now think I should have said more to cover my back on this point, as it evidently presents a difficulty for some readers.

The thing I have been most often quizzed about is something I never imagined would particularly pique readers' interest and is the connection between Jupiter and Melchizedek.[7] Lots and lots of people have written to me about that. I now point them in the direction of this helpful page put together by James O'Fee.[8]

There have been no serious, detailed scholarly interactions with my work, as far as I'm aware, apart from that by Justin Barrett. He subjected my thesis to "quantitative analysis" and I wrote a response to his paper. Both essays were published in the online supplements to *Seven: An Anglo-American Literary Review* and can be

---
[3] Ward, *Planet Narnia*, 232.
[4] Ibid., 64
[5] Ibid., 148.
[6] Ibid., 232.
[7] Ibid., 50.
[8] http://www.impalapublications.com/blog/index.php?/archives/3458-Melchizedek-and-Jupiter,-by-James-OFee.html

read on the website of the Wade Center at Wheaton College (supplements to volumes 27 and 28).[9]

4. Some time after publishing Planet Narnia you began teaching imaginative apologetics at Houston Baptist University. What are the connections (if any) between your work on Planet Narnia and the work you have been doing at HBU?

The main connection is that both in *Planet Narnia* and in my work at HBU I talk about the need for literary atmosphere in imaginative apologetics. Propositional and argumentative apologetics are clearly much needed; they have an important place. But that's not the kind of apologetics I'm principally interested in. I want to emphasize the apologetic value of fiction, poetry, drama, and the vital importance of metaphoric appropriateness and winsome tone in such imaginative works. Christianity is more like a story than it is like an argument, and the best stories have atmospheres and an aesthetic coherence to them, not just a workable plot. In *Phantastes*, the work that "baptised" Lewis's imagination, George MacDonald wrote this: "As the lights and influences of the upper worlds sink silently through the earth's atmosphere . . . so doth Faerie invade the world of men."[10] The same can be said of the effect of Christian fiction and drama and poetry; it can envelop your mind, and heart, and soul, and does so most successfully when it is all-inclusive, paying attention to apparent minutiae and holistic questions of 'flavour' and 'quiddity' and 'quality', as well as sheer narrative logic. Atmosphere is particularly important for serving what Newman called "the illative sense," the faculty we have in

---

[9] https://www.wheaton.edu/academics/academic-centers/wadecenter/publications/vii-journal/contents/online-articles/

[10] George MacDonald, *Phantastes, A Faerie Romance* (Grand Rapids, MI: Eerdmans, 2000), 85.

our minds and souls for apprehending the relevant conditions and determining how best to make inferences in a given situation. Most people don't come to faith under "laboratory conditions"; laboratories are too antiseptic, too artificial for that. Of course, laboratories — and their apologetic equivalents — definitely have their uses, but they are relatively limited, I believe. The rounded, all-encompassing gestalt embrace is what's more usually needed, apologetically or evangelistically speaking, and when a great author manages to communicate that coherent embrace, it can be hugely liberating to the imagination and, as may be, to the intellect and the will and the heart in turn. That's what Lewis in Narnia and Tolkien in Middle-earth achieved so well, and that's why their works are so central to the courses I teach at HBU.

In the case of Narnia, the way in which the children respond to the various manifestations of Aslan, becoming progressively more Jovial, Martial, Solar, etc., is Lewis's attempt to communicate imaginatively the otherwise incommunicable process of learning the divine nature by acquaintance or Enjoyment. Non-Christians, he says:

> cannot be expected to see how the quality of the object which we think we are beginning to know by acquaintance drives us to the view that if this were delusion then we should have to say that the universe had produced no real thing of comparable value ... That is knowledge we cannot communicate.[11]

When he says, "That is knowledge we cannot communicate," I think he means "cannot communicate *directly*." There are some things that have to be

---

[11] C. S. Lewis, "On Obstinacy in Belief," *The Sewanee Review*, accessed December 3, 2018, https://thesewaneereview.com/on-obstinacy-and-belief/.

communicated indirectly or holistically; they can't be reduced to particular, identifiable terms; they won't survive forthright articulation. Nonetheless, we can sense them and be influenced by them, often in very profound ways.

5. In chapter twelve of the book, you describe your 'eureka' moment in nearly mystical terms. You mention, for example, how a musical rendition of The Lion, The Witch, and The Wardrobe *keyed you in to the non-verbal "musicality of the tale," how the subject of wordlessness in a discussion with Rt. Revd. Simon Barrington-Ward charged the atmosphere around you and made it palpable, and how you were so excited the night you read about Jupiter in Lewis's poem that you began pulling books off of the shelves in your pajamas. Ten years later, what are your reflections concerning that set of experiences? Have you a theory on what are the essential ingredients for attaining such insights (spiritual, literary or otherwise)?*

As I reflect on it now, it still strikes me as one of the most significant events of my life. Significant in itself, I mean, quite irrespective of what it led to. At the time, of course, I didn't know all that it would lead to, but immediately after it happened I felt as though I'd been struck by a kind of lightning. I walked around Cambridge in a daze for about two weeks; it was like being concussed — but in a good way!

I watched a documentary a few years ago about the mathematician Andrew Wiles and how he proved Fermat's Last Theorem. As Wiles recounted the moment when he finally realized he'd "got it," he became rather choked up, and I understood exactly what he was feeling. Of course, cracking "the Narnia code" is nothing compared with proving Fermat's Last Theorem, an intellectual puzzle that had stood unsolved for over 350 years, but there's a similarity in kind, if not in degree. When you suddenly see clearly what has baffled you for so long, there's a beauty to it, a blessed relief, a joy. It overwhelms you. In short, it's like an experience of the numinous, and though you can now begin to understand the mystery, you can't understand why it's you who should have first understood it. So it leaves you feeling awe-struck, like Mole and Ratty before Pan.

As for my thoughts on what are the essential ingredients; well, the first thing I'd say is that it's a gift. It's a grace. You couldn't have expected it to happen and you can't count on a similar thing happening again in the future. So it seemed to me then and so it seems to me now. I view this discovery as a Godsend, and accordingly I understand the work it has enabled me to do (this connects with my answer to Question 1) as something of a vocation.

Nevertheless, grace usually builds on nature, and at the natural level, I can now see that there were various foundations that had been lain down over many years that led to the grace-filled moment. First of all, I'd been reading the Chronicles for nearly thirty years, and reading them really attentively, noticing all their idiosyncrasies and peculiarities. Second, I'd been progressively immersing myself in Lewis's total corpus, so that I was becoming more and more familiar with all the contours of his thinking. And third, I'd spent eighteen months examining in depth what he meant by implicit communication, how you say something without saying it directly. So those three things had prepared me, I now realise, to be in the right place at the right time and standing at just the right angle to receive the bolt when the lightning struck.

A friend of mine who used to teach at Wheaton College told me he was once asked by a student how you "go about making a discovery" like this. He answered his student by saying, "You have to love what you're studying. Love is the great opener of eyes." And I think he's right. He's certainly in good company, because Owen Barfield says a very similar thing in *Poetic Diction*: "Love is the begetter of intimate knowledge; for what we love it is not tedious, but delightful, to observe minutely." I had loved what I was studying so much that I wasn't content with a mere superficial understanding; I wanted all it had to give me and I wasn't going to rest till I'd broken through to a deeper level. I'm not saying, of course, that I now thoroughly grasp all that the Chronicles have to offer; there are many things that remain mysterious to me and even what is now clear is still itself, with its own independent integrity, not something I can reduce to a mere toy that I dominate or control by exerting exegetical power over it. One's relationship with a text is like a relationship with a person: only if you love them can you truly get to know them. Without loving them you might know them with *savoir* knowledge (you could know facts about them, all the biographical data), but never would you come to the intimacy that's provided by *connaître* knowledge (knowledge by acquaintance, personal knowing).

6. Most of us at AUJ are completely convinced by your analysis of the Chronicles and C.S. Lewis's 'hidden' imaginative blueprint. But are you still convinced? Would you make any changes if you could? What part of your argument could be strengthened, or where could more work be done, in your view?

I'm in no doubt that Lewis did indeed use the planets as his imaginative blueprint, but yes, I would make a few changes if I were ever to produce a second edition. I would, for instance, make stronger defences against those objections I mentioned above in my answer to Question 3. I would also further develop the case I make in Chapter 11 where I discuss what may have prompted Lewis to write the first Chronicle. I think there's more that can be said to show how Lewis's case against Naturalism may inform *The Lion, the Witch and the Wardrobe*. For example, Lewis did not just argue (in *Miracles* and elsewhere) that naturalism is self-refuting (a point I did make, on page 217), he specifically said that naturalism "cuts its own throat" (see his essay "Religion Without Dogma?"), a line I did not include, but which I now consider extremely telling. In a new edition of *Planet Narnia*, I would draw much more attention to the way Lewis builds up tension in *The Lion, the Witch and the Wardrobe* as the White Witch readies herself to murder Edmund:

> "Prepare the victim," said the Witch. And the dwarf undid Edmund's collar and folded back his shirt at the neck. Then he took Edmund's hair and pulled his head back so that he had to raise his chin. After that Edmund heard a strange noise: whizz - whizz - whizz. For a moment he couldn't think what it was. Then he realized. It was the sound of a knife being sharpened.

We're not told that the Witch intends to cut Edmund's throat; Lewis leaves us to deduce that for ourselves. But how interesting that the Witch plans to kill her victim in this particular fashion, rather than poisoning him, say, or hanging him, or drowning him! It's indicative, I think, of the connection in Lewis's mind between his case against naturalism and the story he's unfolding in Narnia. What he described metaphorically in "Religion Without Dogma?" he here dramatises literally. In turning against Aslan and allying himself with the White Witch, Edmund has adopted the position of a naturalist (so to speak), a position that is self-refuting; it saws off the bough on which it sits. Edmund's rejection of true kingly authority (i.e., the authority represented philosophically by Idealism and theologically by Theism and Christianity, as described in *Miracles*) will result in the cutting of his throat, unless he is saved by the real King of that world — a salvation which of course does indeed happen as Aslan's troops come rushing to his rescue in the nick of time. I think this tell-tale parallel about throat-cutting helps support my contention that *The Lion* is the imaginative re-working of Lewis's argument against naturalism, but I hadn't spotted that link before *Planet Narnia* first came out.

7. What has the response been to Planet Narnia **from creative types (artists, authors, poets, etc.)? Have you been able to see the influence of your own work?**

It's been marvelous how many and various have been the responses. Here are a few of the more notable examples:

The actor, Jamie Parker (now best known for playing the lead role in *Harry Potter and the Cursed Child*), got in touch with me to say that reading *Planet Narnia* had clued him into atmosphere and symbolism in such a way that he now understood much better his role in *As You Like It*, which he was then performing in at Shakespeare's Globe Theatre in London. He later went on to take the title role in *Henry V* and deliberately shaped his performance round the planetary language (e.g. "a largess universal like the Sun") that Shakespeare uses for the King.

The artist, Toni Jessop, was inspired to paint a series of planetary-themed pictures and mounted a three-week exhibition at a gallery in the Blue Mountains west of Sydney, Australia.

The composer, James Whitbourn, wrote a musical portrait of Lewis for the Belfast Philharmonic Choir entitled "The Seven Heavens."[12] Another composer, Joel Clarkson, is working on a setting of Lewis's poem "The Planets" which he plans to premier at The Sheen Center in New York City in 2019. I've been honoured to collaborate with James and Joel on both these projects.

The poet, Malcolm Guite, has not only written a sequence of poems entitled "Seven Heavens, Seven Hells" but has had them set to music by Marty O'Donnell, and both poetry and music have been illustrated in a video sequence that will soon be forthcoming.[13]

Most amusingly, the set-dresser for the BBC's hit television series, *Sherlock*, decided to put a copy of *Planet Narnia* on the bookshelves lining the studio mock-up of 221B Baker Street. (I found out because a keen-eyed viewer took a screenshot of all the books in Holmes's personal library and posted it on Facebook.) Bizarrely, Sherlock likes literary criticism about theologically imaginative uses of medieval cosmology! But as someone pointed out, it's just possible that there is a clever allusion here to what Holmes says to Watson in *The Study in Scarlet*: "You say that we go round the sun. If we went round the moon it would not make a pennyworth of difference to me or to my work."

Of other responses, let me mention just three. First, an Oxford doctoral student wrote to tell me that thinking about Lewis's donegalitarian scheme had brought a whole new perspective to his study of the Old Testament Books of Samuel. Second, a young suitor sent me a copy of the

---

[12] More here: https://vimeo.com/129144613.
[13] Here's a taster of the Moon movement: https://www.youtube.com/watch?v=-mrDRsB6O_0

planetary-themed love-poem he had addressed to his girlfriend shortly before they got engaged (they're now married). Third, and perhaps best of all, an already-married couple notified me that they had named their new-born daughter Jovi, after 'Joviality'. Lewis's love of Jupiter is now not just known by the literati, it has taken flesh and is walking among us on two legs!

An unapologetically orthodox wardrobe.
Image © Lancia E. Smith

"Michael was giving an address to the C.S. Lewis Foundation Summer Institute attendees in 2011."

- Lancia E Smith

Where Paradoxes Play:

Michael Ward on Christian Orthodoxy

Jahdiel Perez

It may be tempting to forget, especially when duly honoring and appraising the impact *Planet Narnia* has had in its first decade, that its author is more than arguably the world's leading C.S. Lewis scholar. Dr. Michael Ward is an intriguing theological thinker in his own right. Though the Narnian shadow of Lewis is a blessed one to be under, Ward's work has emerged from its penumbra and is already casting its own theological influence. This influence is none other than the enchanting touch of orthodoxy itself. His commitment to what Christianity has historically believed and proclaimed is evident not only in the substance of his chapter and epilogue in *Heresies and How to Avoid Them* — a work he co-edited and published the same year as *Planet Narnia* — but also in his very motivation to produce such a book. Of the many interesting theological claims he makes in that work, I would like to explore and unpack how he catalyzes a recovery of vision and appreciation for the paradoxical nature of orthodox Christianity.

Consider what he writes in the following passage of his epilogue:

> Orthodoxy is far too rich, subtle, lively and paradoxical to be reduced to a set of philosophical categories. We must never presume to think that we can suck the heart out of its mystery. To construe it as something apprehensible by the intellect alone would be to suggest that what we're talking about is merely a proposition, something lying inert and analysable in a system of thought. But in reality, Christian orthodoxy, understood properly, is not something that we can fully grasp, still less dissect. Rather, it is a means of keeping ourselves exposed to the truth which grasps us.[1]

Swayed largely by Enlightenment rationalism, theologians and apologists bent on demonstrating the reasonableness of Christian faith have tended to deflate its mysteries. Under the influence of "Cartesian anxiety,"[2] they have developed an allergy to paradoxes, so that the less mysterious, the more rationally appealing Christianity is thought to be. Christian orthodoxy is construed as if it has nothing more or better to offer than intellectual understanding.

Ward invites us to wonder whether Christianity is meant to appeal to more than just the human mind. What if, as Paul Tillich put it, Christian faith involves and therefore ought to appeal to the "total personality," the whole being of a person?[3] After all, is not the Greatest Commandment to love the Lord our God with *everything*; mind but also heart and soul? If this is so, there are other ways Christianity ought to appeal to us than just rationally,

---

[1] Michael Ward, "Epilogue" in *Heresies and How to Avoid Them: Why it Matters what Christians Believe*, eds. Ben Quash and Michael Ward (London: SPCK, 2007), 140.

[2] A phrase coined by philosopher Richard Bernstein, "Cartesian anxiety" refers to the disquieting desire for absolute certainty Descartes entrenched in modern philosophy. See his *Beyond Objectivism and Relativism: Science, Hermeneutics, and Praxis* (Philadelphia: University of Pennsylvania Press, 1983), 16-22.

[3] Paul Tillich, *Dynamics of Faith* (New York: Harper One, 1957), 4-9.

and paradoxes may play a role in making these different forms of appeal possible.

Following G.K. Chesterton, Ward affirms that, far from being logical problems to resolve, paradoxes are the essence of Christian orthodoxy. Sublime mysteries like the three-in-oneness of God and the hypostatic union of Christ make the Christian faith what it is. These living mysteries are irreducible, inextricable and constitutive of the Gospel, so much so that any attempt to reduce them results in not simply misunderstanding but also impoverishment. Whereas rationalist theologians and apologists view a strictly logical account as either a neutral lateral explication of orthodoxy or an elevation of its apparent opaque nonsense to rational transparency, Ward sees this as a reduction of the extravagance, richness, and intricate mystery of orthodoxy that overflows neat philosophical categories.

Intriguingly, Ward observes that heresies are often the product of a desire to avoid paradox. He writes, "the alternative to orthodoxy was always quite plausible, quite attractive, and convincing; it took intellectual effort, moral courage, and political skill to resist it."[4] Heresies make sense; *too much* sense for orthodoxy. To deny the full divinity or humanity of Jesus, as Arianism and Docetism do, is an attempt to circumvent the paradoxical orthodox affirmation that he was fully both. The same goes for Theopaschitism; the heretical belief that the unchangeable divine nature in Jesus can suffer because of its union to his changeable human nature. "By dissolving the mystery," writes Ward, "Theopaschitism makes easy

---

[4] Ward, *Heresies*, 60.

and plausible what in reality is the deepest, most staggering and humbling Christian mystery of all: God, the impassible, suffers as a man."[5] It is difficult to imagine how this truth could appeal to us in a profound, staggering, and humbling manner without its paradoxicality. It is not clear, in other words, that what would remain after excising the paradox is something that would strike us as profoundly astonishing and humbling. Christian orthodoxy affirms the paradox, whereas heresies seek to dissolve it in various ways, rendering what is inherently mysterious into something comfortable and plausible to the natural human mind. In this sense, heresies have something in common with those who seek to present an exclusively rational view of Christianity.[6]

This does not mean that orthodoxy is where unreason runs amok. It does not encourage all or any manner of absurdities. Just as it is possible to make bitter liquid medicine taste worse by, say, adding vinegar to it, it is possible to make the foolishness of God that is the Gospel more offensive to human reason than it necessarily has to be. There are ways to blacken or break the dim glass through which we now see and know in part. To foreground the necessity of paradox in Christian orthodoxy, as Ward does, is no excuse to proliferate mystery in it unnecessarily. Like Lewis, who titled it a "Warning" in his anthology, Ward heeds George MacDonald's exhortation: "We must not wonder things away into nonentity."[7] At the opposite extreme of staunch

---

[5] Ward, *Heresies*, 68.

[6] Influenced by Michael Ward's work with Ben Quash, Josephine Gabelman makes much of this point in her *A Theology of Nonsense* (Eugene, Oregon: Pickwick Publications, 2016), 46-52.

[7] As quoted in C.S. Lewis, *George MacDonald: An Anthology of 365 Readings* (London: Collins, 2016 [1955]), 87.

rationalist theologians and apologists are those who would bloat the essential paradoxes of orthodoxy into exaggerated nonsense. The former deflate the mysteries of orthodoxy, whereas the latter arbitrarily inflate them to the point of nonexistence and irrelevance. We must beware the yeast of both.

But orthodoxy does more than avoid such extremes. It is, writes Ward, "more than the sum of its avoidances."[8] The enticing image that comes to mind is of someone walking straight, balanced between two false extremes, yet remaining ready at any step to dive headlong into the depths of extreme love of God, with all the truth, beauty, and goodness that entails. Nuancing Lewis's comment through Screwtape, that a "moderated religion is as good for us as no religion at all,"[9] Ward states that we need "moderation in all things, including moderation! If we think that balance is the be-all and end-all we will be selling orthodoxy short, for there is such a thing as excessive balance."[10] We can imagine that now: a man so obsessed with being perfectly balanced that his gaze is fixed downward to his feet so that his stiff gait barely moves forward. Ward adds, "this unnatural symmetry, this calculated colonization of the dead-point between two transmitters, this insistent compromise, is robotic."[11] Indeed, experience may confirm that intense, exclusive concentration tends to hinder rather than help our bodies balance things in our hands. It is as if the body can balance better when narrow mental concentration gets slightly out of its way. So too with the body of Christ that is the

---

[8] Ward, *Heresies*, 131.
[9] C.S. Lewis, *The Screwtape Letters* (New York: HarperCollins, 1996 [1942]), 46.
[10] Ward, *Heresies*, 134.
[11] Ibid., 134-135.

Church. It moves freely and naturally forward, balanced much better among extremes, when its eyes are fixed upward on Jesus, ready to love and worship him with everything. As Ward puts it, "Orthodoxy is a matter of the heart and soul, not just of balance."[12]

The very word 'orthodoxy,' especially today, is stalked by a "horror of the Same Old Thing," which Screwtape describes as "one of the most valuable passions we have produced in the human heart — an endless source of heresies in religion…"[13] Familiarity produces contempt in so many people who think the old truths of orthodoxy are old news. Ward's vision of the paradoxical nature of Christian orthodoxy is better equipped to overcome this obstacle and gain a fresh hearing among audiences today. Mystery tends to resist over-familiarity, incite curiosity, and discourage contempt. Ward invites the mysteries of Christian orthodoxy to shine forth. His view of orthodoxy reopens a wardrobe into a world where paradoxes play and keep us "exposed to the truth which grasps us." What could be more fascinating than that?

---

[12] Ward, *Heresies*, 135.
[13] Lewis, *Screwtape*, 135.

WHY WE LOVE TO VISIT NARNIA

Louis Markos

A full decade has now passed since Michael Ward published his groundbreaking *Planet Narnia*. While remaining faithful to the full Christian meanings of the Chronicles, Ward skillfully factored in a third layer of meaning that demonstrated to adoring fans and skeptical naysayers alike that Lewis's Narnia books were built on a firm but flexible literary foundation. Far from the helter-skelter grab-bag that Tolkien, alas, thought them to be, *The Chronicles of Narnia* embody a consistent vision grounded in the seven planets of the Medieval cosmological model: a model that Lewis himself magisterially described in *The Discarded Image*.

According to that model, each of the seven "planets" (Greek for "wanderer") — Moon, Mercury, Venus, Sun, Mars, Jupiter, Saturn — shed its influence upon our stationary yet fickle world. Thus, while the moon produced silver in the earth and inspired lunacy in men and the Sun produced gold and made men wise and generous. Mars and Jupiter drew forth, respectively, iron and a martial spirit and tin and a jovial spirit. The Medievals believed this planetary influence was imprinted on our terrestrial air; hence, our word "influenza," which was thought to be spread, like the plague, by bad air.

The genius of Ward's thesis and book is the way it reveals in rich detail how each of the seven Chronicles shows forth the manifold influences of one of the seven planets. When we read, say, *The Lion, the Witch and the Wardrobe*, we not only come face to face with the Christ of Narnia; we immerse ourselves in the jovial influence of the planet Jupiter. As such, we experience Aslan simultaneously as the sacrificed-and-risen King of Narnia and as the supreme fountainhead of joviality. By climbing aboard *The Voyage of the Dawn Treader*, readers partake in an adventure where temptations must be met with Christian virtues, but they also participate in a dazzling solar influence that slays dragons, promotes liberality, and brings intellectual clarification and spiritual illumination.

Ward is right, I am convinced, that Lewis consciously infused his Chronicles with the influences of the seven Medieval planets. And he is right, as well, that that infusion gives the Chronicles much of their universal appeal. But I would suggest that the appeal of Narnia — what makes readers love it so dearly and desire to revisit it again and again — goes a bit deeper: It is not just the imaginative link between the seven Chronicles and the seven planets that makes readers yearn to pass through the wardrobe. It is the fact that Narnia is a Medieval place where such things as influence are operative.

The Chronicles invite us to enter a world that is wonderful and meaningful: that is to say, full of wonder and filled with meaning. In Narnia, neither the planets, nor the stars, nor all the myriad of heavenly bodies are cold, distant, and aloof. When Othello exclaims that it is "the very error of the moon; / She comes more nearer earth than she was wont, / And makes men mad,"[1] he says something that should disturb and frighten us. But it should inspire us as well with a deeper sense of numinous awe. Could it be that there is a true link, an intimate connection between the heavens and the earth, between the macrocosm around us and the microcosm within us? Could the universe really be like that?

The cause of that insidious malaise, that soul-crushing existential angst that has fallen over the western world is twofold. Not only has modern man rejected the traditional belief that we are born with a God-given essence that defines, shapes, and guides us; he has rejected as well any sense that we live in a sympathetic universe. Oh, he will often make an idol of nature, even going so far as to privilege nature over human wellbeing, but he will not therefore treat her as an older, equally fallen sister fashioned by the same loving Creator. As Lewis's fellow Inkling, Owen Barfield argued in his *Saving the Appearances*, our post-Enlightenment world has turned nature into an object, a thing to be studied rather than a fellow creature to be loved.

Our Newtonian, clockwork universe has been robbed of its glory and its mystery. But not Narnia. There, in Lewis's restored Medieval cosmos, everything, from larches to lakes, beavers to badgers, stars to salamanders, is alive with meaning. It's not just that the animals can talk. It's that Narnia is a world where talking animals do not seem

---
[1] Shakespeare. *Othello*. 5.2.135.

strange or out of place. According to a Medieval legend, on the night Christ was born in Bethlehem, the animals were given the power of speech. If that is true, then Narnia is a place where it is, in fact, always Christmas! True, witches (whether white or green) and tyrants (whether Telmarine or Calormene) might silence them for a season, but they cannot wholly extinguish their voices. Jesus once said that if the multitude refused to bless his name, the rocks themselves would cry out. Narnia is a place where the whole shimmering cosmos cries out with praise, gratitude, and an affirmation of the goodness of life.

As readers of Narnia, we don't just want to study or witness that shimmering cosmos. We want to enter in to it. Even so, in his greatest sermon, "The Weight of Glory," Lewis says that our true desire, the one we can barely put into words, is not just to see the beauty of nature but to be united with it, "to pass into it, to receive it into ourselves, to bathe in it, to become part of it."[2] Narnia offers us that longed-for opportunity. There, we can dine with talking beavers, dance with living trees, and speak with animated rivers. We can even hold conversations with valiant mice, liberated gnomes, and paroled stars.

When young Prince Caspian fears that the Narnian versions of Mars and Venus will bump into each other in their majestic trek across the heavens, his wise, half-dwarf tutor Doctor Cornelius assures him that the "great lords of the upper sky know the steps of their dance too well for that."[3] When rash King Rilian insists that Aslan has returned, the wise, prophetic Centaur Roonwit tells him

---

[2] C.S. Lewis, "The Weight of Glory," *The Weight of Glory and Other Addresses*, (San Francisco: Harper Collins, 2001), 42.

[3] C.S. Lewis, *Prince Caspian* (New York: HarperCollins, 2001), 338.

that if "Aslan were really coming to Narnia, the sky would have foretold it. If he were really come, all the most gracious stars would be assembled in his honor."[4] When Eustace insists that a star is nothing but "a huge ball of flaming gas," the wise, retired star Ramandu explains that even in his terrestrial world, "that is not what a star is but only what it is made of."[5]

We who love Narnia are like Shasta in the opening chapter of The Horse and His Boy. We have grown weary of our faithless, hopeless, loveless existence and long to escape to a world where there is true joy and freedom and purpose. We may even find in ourselves a strange urge to look at a horse and confess to it our secret wish that it could talk. That, of course, is what Shasta does, only to have Bree respond that he can talk and that he is prepared to journey with him to that mythic land up north that Shasta has always dreamed of visiting. There, Shasta believes, he can live life in a fuller, richer way.

Narnia, like heaven in Lewis's The Great Divorce, offers not so much a larger space as a larger *kind* of space where one can escape from the cramped limits of our cold, cynical, disenchanted world. The divine music out of which Narnia was born still echoes in the grass and the streams and the trees. Even during the hundred year reign of the White Witch, the Narnians remember their true heritage and tell tales about "midnight dances and how the Nymphs who lived in the wells and the Dryads who lived in the trees came out to dance with the Fauns."[6] The magic can be suppressed, but it cannot be obliterated.

---

[4] C.S. Lewis, The Last Battle (New York: HarperCollins, 2001), 676.
[5] The Voyage of the Dawn Treader (New York: HarperCollins, 2001), 522.
[6] C.S. Lewis, The Lion, the Witch, and the Wardrobe (New York: HarperCollins, 2001), 116-117.

In *The Silver Chair*, the Green Witch tries to convince our heroes that there is no such thing as the sun or lions, that they have made them up by imagining a bigger torch or a bigger cat. In the same way, our modern schools and colleges have striven mightily to convince their charges that the supernatural world is nothing more than a child's tale, an emotional wish fulfillment for people who can't handle the real world. But our heroes know better. They agree, with Puddleglum, that the Witch's clockwork, materialistic universe can't hold a candle to their so-called play world, and they are prepared to risk all to reach that better world. They know they will likely die in the search, but the true Narnians consider that "small loss if the world's as dull a place" as the Witch claims.[7]

Readers who love Narnia love it tenaciously. They will not allow a hollow rationalism or scientism to rob them of the magic that runs rampant from Lantern Waste to Cair Paravel, reaching out its strong but supple fingers to take in the northern wastes, the uncharted eastern sea, and the barren deserts of the south. Freud, Marx, and Darwin, like Dennett, Hitchens, and Dawkins, may have stripped the wonder away from our world, but they cannot strip us of our desire to live in a sympathetic, God-haunted cosmos.

In *The Magician's Nephew*, Queen Jadis brags of her skill for destroying worlds. Like Screwtape, she is adept at removing music and silence and replacing it with noise. But she cannot undo the goodness, truth, and beauty of Narnia. Just so, the naturalism of our modern age cannot darken the light of Narnia; rather, it is the Narnian light that exposes our darkness. Digory learns as much when he

---

[7] C.S. Lewis, *The Silver Chair* (New York: HarperCollins, 2001), 222.

brings a Narnian apple to London: "The brightness of the Apple threw strange lights on the ceiling. Nothing else was worth looking at: indeed you couldn't look at anything else. And the smell of the Apple of Youth was as if there was a window in the room that opened on Heaven."[8]

My thanks to Michael Ward for helping us to glimpse that heaven a bit more clearly.

---

[8] C.S. Lewis, *The Magician's Nephew* (New York: HarperCollins, 2001), 104.

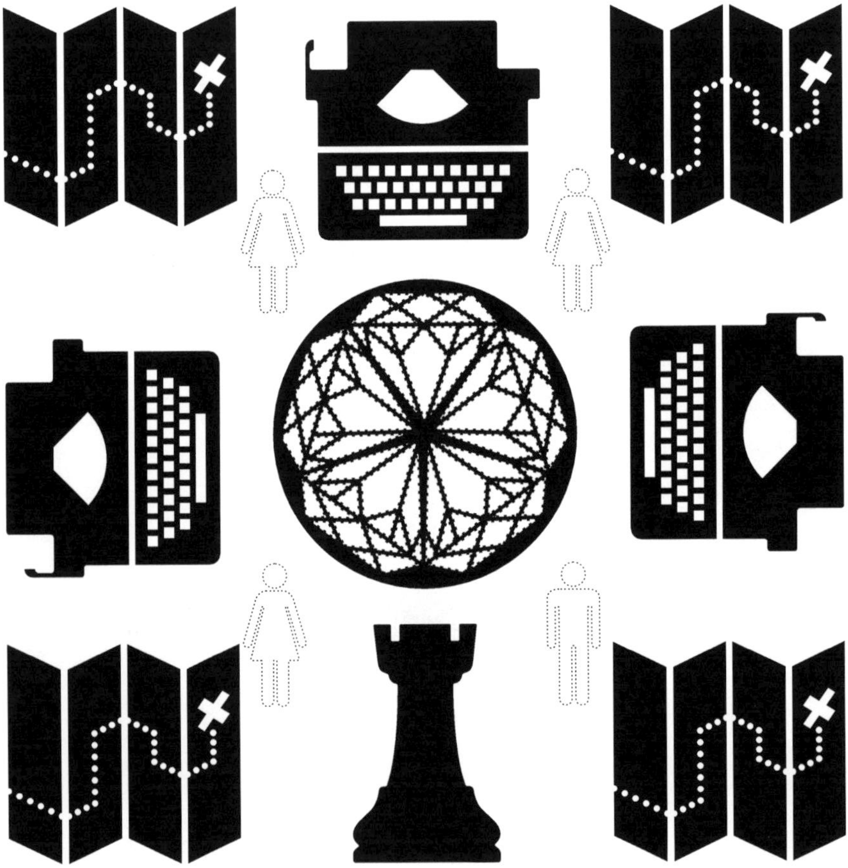

An Unexpected Journey:

Imaginative Apologetics and the Ward Moment -
A Personal Reflection

John Mark Reynolds

In an issue honoring a remarkable scholar, I have been asked to do two things: honor the scholar and tell how Apologetics and Michael Ward came to Houston Baptist University. This requires saying something about *why* cultural apologetics was (with cinema and new media) such a priority for me during my time at HBU.

Michael Ward was a major part of answering a question I had all my life about education: how can we continue what Lewis and Tolkien started? In God's good grace he was an answer that came with *many other wonderful people that keep giving a fuller answer to that question.*

Ward is a churchman, not much celebrated as a category just now, but that means he is a man of community: living and dead. To know Michael Ward is to know the Church, humble and glorious. How did I meet him?

The right question came first, as must be, if anything good is to come.

Just a Bus Ride: Plato, Tolkien, and a Kid

Imagine finding *Lord of the Rings* in the library in seventh grade, opening it on the bus ride home, looking up to the rainy window, and knowing you had lost your weekend! Narnia already had captured my heart as my brother and I did what many children do, bump into the back of closets looking for other worlds. Tolkien ended any chance that the scientism of another writer I loved, Isaac Asimov, would harden my heart.

I wanted wonderful science and sensible wonder: Lewis and Tolkien showed this was possible.

Around the same time, I ran into Plato, and made a foolish mistake. The dialogues were *brilliant*, but as a kid I assumed the thing to do was to memorize the responses! I could then deploy them in the proper situations, yet the proper situations never came. Upstate New York turned out to have a shortage of ancient Athenian people who share the assumptions of Plato's characters!

This taught me a lesson: *arguments are for people, not people for arguments*. Imagination can quickly jump several steps through intuition and see what later can be confirmed through careful arguments. *That Hideous Strength* saw the future: providing the arguments simply took time.

That bus ride and my later experiences in education left me dissatisfied. Lewis and Tolkien were gone to glory. Where was their like? Less ambitiously: where were people who would fill out the imaginative apologetics they pioneered? Couldn't we have analytic philosophy and Narnia too?

I was waiting for people like Michael Ward, but I did not know it at the time.

An Unexpected Journey

If you love Jesus and have an imaginative turn, then apologetics follows. Understanding the Faith can be helpful to outsiders, sometimes, but essential to believers. We see the True Light, now what do we make of this wonder. How does it impact all of reality? Tolkien and Lewis (with some others) did not limit where the Light could shine: every corner of the cosmos, including the imaginative ones, should be bathed in Light.

If I could not do this work myself, could I provide a place for others? Where were they?

When asked to be Provost at Houston Baptist University, I immediately suggested a program in apologetics, but one that was very different. Leadership had, with justification, thought of apologetics as passé, but were open to something different and cultural apologetics was, just then, something completely different!

How could this new apologetics program work?

First, the central focus would not be on philosophy (though philosophy would not be ignored). HBU had a fine graduate program in philosophy long before I came. Integrating the rest of the disciplines, too often ignored in traditional American Apologetics was the goal, instead of an over focus on philosophy and biological sciences. My dream was that apologetics would integrate the totality of the university: the True Light spread to every field.

Second, the time was long past to bring different personality types into apologetics. Could a musician be an apologist? Of course! Where were the band kids grown up? What of the poets? Apologetic audiences seemed to be overwhelmingly engineers at the time.

Third, scholarship and training were often light in apologetics. Could we increase rigor? You cannot get the next C.S. Lewis without robust training. The model apologists in philosophy had such training, but there were few role models in other fields.

Finally, women obviously could do all kinds of work from analytic philosophy to poetry. Why was apologetics too often missing half the human race?

We would, I hoped, offer *cultural apologetics* at HBU.

Who would join this unexpected journey?

Apologetics as a Master Discipline: A Wider Field

There were three people I *knew* could change everything, do more than I could ever do if they got the chance: Mary Jo Sharp, Holly Ordway, and Nancy Pearcey. They agreed to come onboard and having described the general vision, my job was to get out of the way and hope I could teach a class or two!

Like, Plato thought, is attracted to like and so the excellent thinkers, eager to apply imagination and reason to all fields, made things greater than I could have imagined. Hiring Michael Ward was *essential*, but I did not know it.

Professor Holly Ordway, who was a leader from the first, did know it.

Professor Ordway had been an outstanding student in a Masters of Apologetics class on Cultural Apologetics at Biola University and a scholar and professor in her own field of English literature. Through Professor Ordway and also through the C.S. Lewis Foundation, I knew Professor Ward in the sense one admires one's betters!

Ordway suggested that maybe, just maybe, Ward would journey with us. The trick was how? Nobody wanted Ward to leave Oxford, not Ward, and not me. This is where a rethink of *online* was key. Too many had made online a way to dilute the contact of students with professors. What if instead the tools of online education made geography more negotiable and allowed small classes *and* more discipleship?

Instead of being massive, *online* could be intimate: students drawn globally to a professor who would teach personally. Technology could annihilate space and allow for class to take place between an opera singer in California and Michael Ward in Oxford!

That was my rough idea and Professor Ordway made it possible using the tools we had. Since *incarnation* is important to Christians, this could be blended with weeks where students could spend time with Professor Ward in Houston.

That was the vision, Ordway made it practical and so possible, and to my delight Ward agreed.

Suddenly, we had one of the leading Lewis experts joining a jolly band on a journey to imaginative apologetics. We needed Ward badly, more than I knew.

Professor Ward as Model

This side of *Planet Narnia* and almost a decade of teaching, Ward seems an obvious leader of imaginative apologetics.

Why?

He has taken the True Light further into the cosmos. He has brightened the corners that Lewis and Tolkien promised could be redeemed.

First, he is philosophically and theological astute, but he is not limited to those fields. Ward can read a text and see literary truth. *Planet Narnia* is a brilliant work, even to those who do not agree with the central thesis. This is the surest measure of a good idea: critics love wresting with the concept.

Second, Michael Ward is *not* the typical apologist. He has a poetic turn and an ability to hear the music and not just the lyrics of a work. He is able to see the True Light and has the ability to bear witness to that light even in Westminster Abbey.

Third, Ward is a genuine scholar. He worked hard and earned the proper credentials. He did this without forgetting his roots. He is no "fan boy," but a scholar who read, thought, and explicated. This is vanishingly rare.

Finally, Michael Ward promotes a joyous range of scholars. He is *mere Christian, in a forgotten sense of that abused term*. Ward is a man of the Roman Catholic Church. He is not weak in his beliefs, but the very strength of his convictions allows him to make allies where he can.

There is no shock that a diverse company of wanderers would find this man of wonder.

I have had a long career with more than one unexpected journey. One of the best was the unexpected journey of a cultural apologetics program at a Baptist university and a key reason for the jollification was Michael Ward.

Thank you for existing, Professor Ward.

Holly Ordway and Michael Ward

A SEVEN-DAYS' JOURNEY THROUGH THE HEAVENS

Holly Ordway

We muddle through this world tempest-tossed,
Beleaguered by distractions here below,
And fearing we can't find the way; we're lost

Unless, until, and if a word can show
A glimpse, a hint, a glimmering in the mind
That urges us to move, to seek, to know

The root and ground of love. For here we find
Our Maker does not leave His work half done,
But brings forth life and growth by His design.

The light that brings forth life has also won
The victory over death: the dragon-slayer
Whose work in this dark age is never done . . .

And so we too are called to fight: to pray,
That we may persevere - though we are weak -
To harden wills to serve Our Lord each day.

Indeed he calls us to him, week by week:
To celebrate with joy and festal song
The King of kings among us, hidden, meek . . .

The one who bore the Cross for all our wrongs,
The King of life, who died, and reigns alive,
The one who calls us Home where we belong.

Michael Ward and Malcolm Guite
Image © Lancia E. Smith

Michael and Malcolm stopped for a quick portrait together at the 2011 C.S. Lewis Foundation Summer Institute outside of Great St. Mary's in Oxford.

- Lancia E Smith

Planet Narnia As Creative Inspiration

Malcolm Guite

Like so many other readers of Ward's magnum opus, I have found in *Planet Narnia* a great work of literary criticism, an account of Lewis's works that sends me back to the originals with renewed insight and delight. But over the decade since its publication, I have come to realize that it offers something more than that. *Planet Narnia* turns out to be a book about much more than the Narniad, or about the seven heavens, or even about the truth of imagination; it is also a book about the art of writing.

Ward shows how Lewis relished, and wished to capture in his writing, the intrinsic and distinctive quality of people and places, even of books, which Lewis called 'Donegality' — a private word derived from his sense that there was something distinctive about Donegal that differentiated it from the rest of Ireland: its 'Donegality'. What Lewis wanted as a writer was to give each of his chronicles a unique 'Donegality', a flavour and atmosphere of its own, and through that distinction to make each of his books the "local habitation" for distinctive but elusive spiritual qualities which might otherwise drift past us as an "airy nothing."

What Ward demonstrates is that, rather than invent a private language or symbolic system, Lewis availed himself of what was already "out there" (quite literally): the discarded image, the long-neglected lore and poetry, the symbolic system of the seven heavens. By working with these 'given', indeed archetypal symbolic systems, Lewis was essentially working collaboratively. He was effectively summoning Dante and Spenser to his side, drawing from them, conversing with them, and re-tuning their resonance to harmonise his own particular work. Paradoxically it is this very collaboration which set free in Lewis the creative flair and originality which has given his work its distinctive flavour and its staying power.

This approach to the art of writing is entirely consistent with his critical theory, his defence of Stock Responses against I. A. Richards, and his brilliant analysis of how Milton achieved his effects by drawing on what was already 'given' in his own sources, the Bible and Virgil. Lewis is not so much working as a private isolated writer making his own separate creation but more as a mediæval mason adding to, enlarging, and gracing with detail a much bigger 'cathedral' of poetry and symbol which is the ongoing work of many hands and many generations. This is not only a good account of poets in the past, it is good news for contemporary poets and writers in other genres too.

Looking back on my own writing practice since I read *Planet Narnia*, I realise I have been emboldened and encouraged to draw more freely and frankly on the clusters of symbol and meaning, the beautifully articulated emblems which are our common inheritance, and especially on those planetary symbols which are the subject of Planet Narnia.

In particular, there are two poems in my collection *The Singing Bowl*, which I think could not have been written in the way they were without the inspiration of *Planet Narnia*. I am happy to offer them afresh in this *Festschrift*, with a grateful acknowledgement of Michael Ward's role in preparing my mind to write them.

The first, "The Daily Planet," is playful lyric, but with perhaps a more serious undertone, which takes the tropes around Venus and Mars and voices them for relations between the sexes, influenced, among other things by Ward's reading of Lewis's Cosmic Trilogy in which a 'Mars' book is followed by a 'Venus' book and then the two are tied together in a third book whose opening word is 'Matrimony'.

The second is a 'solar' poem from my sequence "On Reading the Commedia," a sequence of nine poems in *terza rima* offering a 'reader response' to Dante's *Divine Comedy*. The eighth poem in that sequence, responds to the 'Solar' Cantos in the *Paradiso*, the cantos in which Dante meets the philosophers and theologians, amongst them Boethius, Bonaventure, and Aquinas. My response is set not in the fourth Heaven but in contemporary Cambridge and describes what it has been like to delight in discovery and to avail myself of the consolations of philosophy. My encounters with Michael Ward in person in Cambridge as well as in print have been part of that delight in discovery, and I am happy to dedicate both of these poems to him now.

THE DAILY PLANET

Malcolm Guite

All day the noise of battle rolls,
The skirmishes and wars,
What peace or treaty can there be
Between two worlds like ours?

Could I be lost in Venus,
Could you be found in Mars,
Then I might search your tender wounds
And you my battle scars,
Then you might pull me from my sphere
Or fall to me from yours,
Were I, perchance, in Venus
And you, perhaps, in Mars.

What wary orbits we must keep
Around our dying sun,
Falling towards the verge of sleep
When all our wars are done,
Falling towards the verge of sleep
Where, lying side by side,
The angels of our planets weep
To see two worlds collide.[1]

---

[1] Malcolm Guite *The Singing Bowl*, (Canterbury Press 2013), p.36.

CIRCLE DANCE

Malcolm Guite

A sun-warmed sapling, opening each leaf,
My soul unfolded in your quickening ray.
"The inner brought the outer into life,"

I found the light within the light of day,
The Consolation of Philosophy,
Turning a page in Cambridge, found my way,

My mind delighting in discovery,
As love of learning turned to learning love
And explanation deepened mystery,

Drawing me out beyond what I could prove
Towards the next adventure. Every chance
Discovery a sweet come-hither wave,

Philosophy a kind of circle dance,
Weaving between the present and the past,
The whole truth present in a single glance

That looked on me and everything in Christ!
Threefold beholding, look me into being,
Make me in Love again from first to last,

And let me still partake your holy seeing
Beyond the shifting shadow of the earth;
Minute particulars, eternal in their being,

Forming themselves into a single path
From heaven to earth and back again to heaven,
All patterned and perfected, from each birth

To each fruition, and all freely given
To glory in and give the glory back!
Call me again to set out from this haven

And follow truth along her shining track.[1]

---

[1] Malcolm Guite, *The Singing Bowl* (London: Canterbury Press, 2013), 122-123.

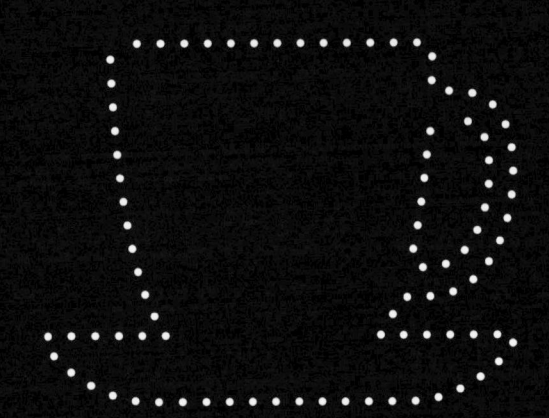

"You can't get a cup of tea large enough or a book long enough to suit me."

— C. S. Lewis to Walter Hooper, reported in Hooper's preface to the Lewis collection *Of Other Worlds: Essays and Stories*

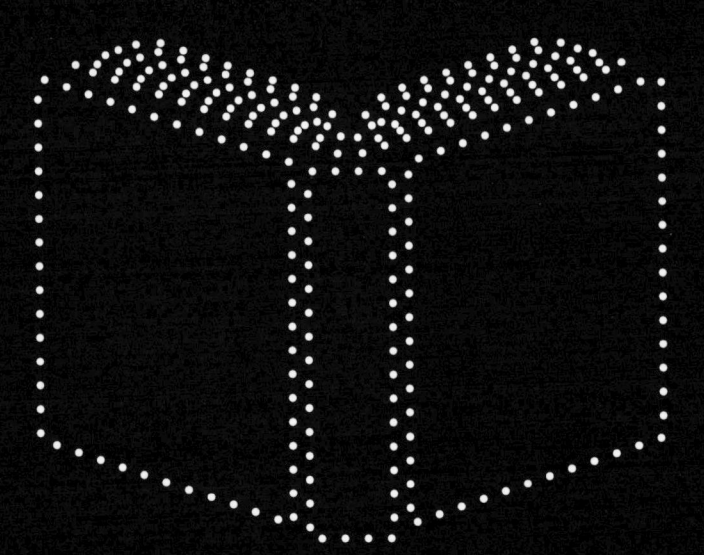

C. S. LEWIS: A LIFE

Donald T. Williams

Such a tapestry his mind could weave;
He gave us Puddleglum and Reepicheep!
Yet there were two things he could not conceive:
A book too long, a pot of tea too deep.

He plumbed the deepest caves of human thought;
He climbed the peaks of poetry and song,
Yet never could he find that God had wrought
A cup of tea too large, a book too long.

Each day would dawn to the same set of plans:
Chapel, breakfast, and then what comes next?
The endless quest to satisfy the man's
Voracious appetite for tea and text.

He gave his time, his energy, his love
To pupils, letters, books, and family,
To friends, chores, God—and the fulfillment of
His endless appetite for text and tea.[1]

---

[1] This poem is taken from the book *Stars Through the Clouds: The Collected Poetry of Donald T. Williams, 2nd ed.* (Lynchburg: Lantern Hollow Press, 2018), and is used here by permission.

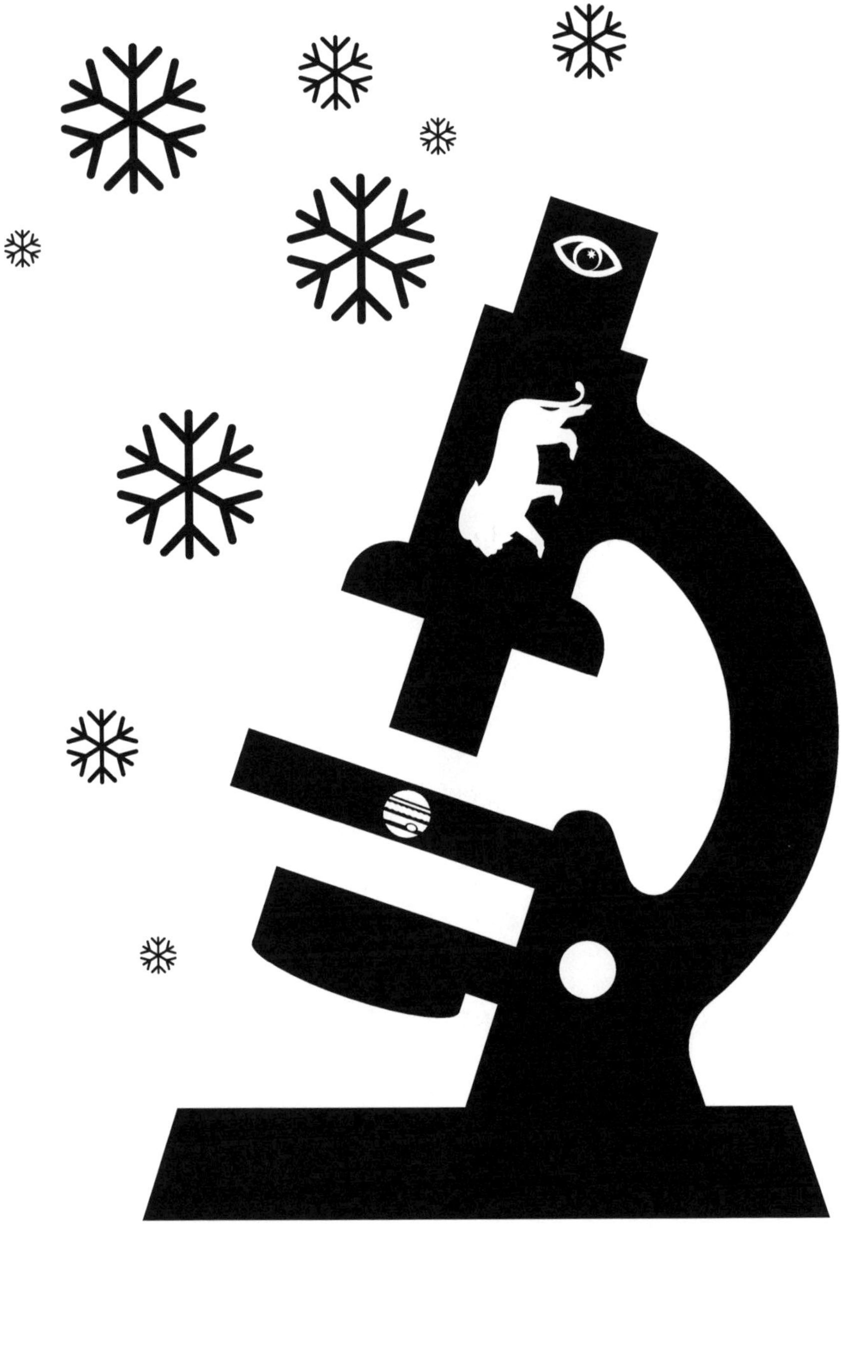

(Re)Considering the Planet Narnia Thesis

Brenton Dickieson

The "Nova Effect" of the Planet Narnia Thesis[1]

With mainstream media attention, a BBC documentary, star-studded podcasts and interviews, and a constellation of books and resources, is there a literary phenomenon quite like Michael Ward's ideas about the medieval genesis of Narnia? Speaking as a C.S. Lewis scholar, I would go so far as to say that *Planet Narnia* is the most important resource for reading *The Chronicles of Narnia* published in this century, creating something like a nova effect in Narnian studies.

Despite my assertion that this is an essential book, I am part of a quiet but not immaterial set of readers who have serious questions about the *Planet Narnia* thesis. I hope you have read and know Ward's book well; however, I want to offer some suggestions on why I think he is wrong. These thoughts are merely teasers, intended to stir constructive and critical conversation. More than anything,

---

[1] For nova effects in worldviews see the epilogue of C.S. Lewis, *The Discarded Image: An Introduction to Medieval and Renaissance Literature* (Cambridge: Canto Classics, 1994), 216-223.

reconsidering the *Planet Narnia* thesis in this way leads to an even greater appreciation of the value of the work.

Put briefly, *Planet Narnia* argues that Lewis intentionally structured the seven Narnian chronicles around the seven planets of medieval cosmology, so that each 'star' influenced a particular book in character development, word play, symbolic layering, Christological imagery, biblical intertextuality, and central theme. Lewis used medieval cosmology not only for imagistic interest or narrative energy, but carefully structured the Narniad around the seven planets. Moreover, he kept that sophisticated design a secret for his entire life, intentionally cloaking the central organizing feature of the Narniad.

I will test the different points of the thesis, defending aspects of it while suggesting new ways to approach *Planet Narnia*.

"The Supreme Medieval Work of Art"[2]

Setting aside text evidence and secrecy for a moment, is the thesis even plausible? I do think there is an inherent plausibility built into the thesis — but it is circular.

If Lewis used medieval forms to create his contemporary fiction, then there is a beautiful synchronicity to Lewis's use of the planetary model. As Lewis argues in *The Discarded Image*, the medieval poets and writers were systematizers. They not only created these grand, beautiful, intricate systems, but also weaved the structured features of their worldview into the complex literary tapestries of their imagination. As Lewis wrote,

---

[2] Lewis, *The Discarded Image*, 12.

"The planets are not merely present ... but woven into the plot."[3] Medieval poets thought integrating the symmetry of the cosmos into art was beautiful and rich, so Lewis's weaving of the medieval model in his Narnian plot would reflect that particular charm.

If Lewis used the medieval model he certainly had a good reason to. We must admit that this is a circular argument. As such, Lewis's love of medieval cosmology only opens up possibilities, as they would in creating a thesis about other things he loved (classical poetry, biblical myth, Celtic folklore, allegorical poetry, epic, etc.).

"Hidden Under 'A Pious Veil of Figments'"?[4]

Moreover, the thesis is based on what Lewis has hidden from the world. There is no external text evidence that we can use to test the thesis.[5] Quite the opposite, in fact. Lewis himself claimed there *was* a structure to *The Chronicles of Narnia* — namely, biblical and Christological typologies that he shared with readers[6] — and that the Narniad was *not* planned ahead of time.[7] Ward's thesis stands in contradistinction to the text evidence we have, and newly released letters shows Lewis slowly working out

---

[3] Lewis, *The Discarded Image*, 201.

[4] Ibid., 65.

[5] "I am not claiming to have unearthed a hitherto unknown document in which Lewis divulged this secret, nor am I relying on previously unpublished testimony from one of his friends or relatives." Michael Ward, *Planet Narnia: The Seven Heavens in the Imagination of C.S. Lewis* (Oxford: Oxford University Press, 2008), 5.

[6] e.g., see the 5 Mar 1961 letter to Anne Jenkins, Walter Hooper, ed. *The Collected Letters of C.S. Lewis: Vol. 3: Narnia, Cambridge, and Joy 1950-1963*, ed. Walter Hooper (New York: HarperSanFrancisco, 2007), 1244-5. Two works that take this note seriously include Charles A. Huttar, "C.S. Lewis's Narnia and the 'Grand Design'" in *The Long for a Form: Essays on the Fiction of C.S. Lewis*, ed., Peter J. Schakel (Kent, OH: Kent State University Press, 1977), 119-35; Will Vaus, *The Hidden Story of Narnia: A Book-by-Book Guide to C.S. Lewis's Spiritual Themes* (Cheshire, CT: Winged Lion Press, 2010).

[7] e.g., see the 21 Apr 1957 letter to Laurence Krieg, CLIII 847-8.

the Narniad over time.[8] Intriguingly, because of the secrecy nature of the thesis, even if we could use textual evidence to support it — if Lewis told someone about his plan — then the thesis falls.

Between the circularity of the idea of Lewis's use of the model and the secrecy element of the thesis, the claim is effectively non-falsifiable. In public talks and lectures, Ward challenges the skeptic to consider his thesis based on the evidence, suggesting that because the evidence is so strong it is up to the reader to disagree.[9] While the intertextual evidence is available for everyone to consider, with the secrecy thesis the reality is the reverse. Using Lewis's own approach to evidence-based analysis we see that, a "theory which could never by any experience be falsified can for that reason hardly be verified."[10]

The *Planet Narnia* thesis is thus non-falsifiable. Ward is rejecting what Lewis actually said about his project, and we can never prove that Lewis *didn't have* a secret plan for the project. *Since the thesis cannot be proved false it can hardly be proved true.*

Moreover, Ward's reason for rejecting Lewis's own testimony about the project is insufficient for three reasons.

First, when Ward suggests Narnia is not just "about Christ" and that Christological books "make up less than

---

[8] See Brenton Dickieson, "A New C.S. Lewis Letter with Details About Narnia," *A Pilgrim in Narnia*, September 12, 2018, accessed November 20, 2018, https://apilgriminnarnia.com/2018/09/12/new-lewis-letter/.

[9] e.g., Michael Ward, Introduction to a new audio course, "Christology, Cosmology, and C.S. Lewis," Now You Know Media Inc., 2017.

[10] The context is about liberal Christianity and sin, but the language of discovery is illustrative: some "would tell us to go on rummaging and scratching till we find something specific.... I think they are right in saying that if we hunt long enough we shall find, or think we have found, something. But that is just what wakens suspicion. A theory which could never by any experience be falsified can for that reason hardly be verified." C.S. Lewis, *Letters to Malcolm: Chiefly on Prayer* (London: Goeffrey Bles, 1964), 50.

half the sequence,"[11] his frame is too narrow. If we follow Lewis in extending the theme to Christ as the prime model for spiritual life, we can see how Narnia is "about Christ."[12]

Second, Ward is right in resisting complaint about Narnia's "hodge-podge" nature. Lewis was, after all, a logically coherent and imaginatively complex thinker, deeply rooted in speculative fiction and an expert in the formation of symbolically laden fictional worlds. However, the whole frame of the question is wrong. Why do we think that drawing from dozens of various biblical, classical, folk, and fictional sources is poor writing? The whole question is based on a modern assumption of authorial originality that Lewis himself rejected, preferring to view himself as part of a tradition of literature, like the latest architect to work on a Norman cathedral.

Third, neither of these claims, even if we granted them, mean that there should be a "scheme," a single structured framework of thought that is the imaginative foundation of the whole. Medieval authors themselves use far more subtle and variant structures than one-to-one planetary allegiances. There may be a sevenfold structure to the Narniad, and I think Ward's work is interesting as a lens for reading, but there is no reason we should expect such a structure.

---

[11] Ward, *Planet Narnia*, 12.

[12] My work argues that this motif is all through Lewis; see Brenton D.G. Dickieson, "'Die Before You Die': St. Paul's Cruciformity in C.S. Lewis" in *Both Sides of the Wardrobe: C.S. Lewis, Theological Imagination and Everyday Discipleship*, ed. Rob Fennell (Eugene, OR: Wipf & Stock, 2015), 32-45.

"The Wise Man Will Over-Rule the Star"[13]

Because of the nature of Ward's claim, it is not up to readers to consider the thesis but for Ward to convince us that there is reason to consider a non-falsifiable thesis. Lewis's own comments and approaches to literary criticism work against this, so I reject the intentional framing of the thesis. And I set aside his claim for a seven book/seven planet linkage until I see the evidence as a whole.

Still, because his work has been so influential and so many stellar scholars have endorsed it, I believe it is worth taking up the other side for a moment. Many people have deep concerns about the conspiratorial nature of the work, which I have demonstrated is non-confirmable. We should consider the skeptic's instinct to cut the thesis off here at the methodological root. A skeptic might say, "in the thousands of scraps we have from Lewis, there is not even an offhand remark about medieval cosmology shaping the series; moreover, there are specific comments about the series representing other kinds of structures." I have shown that these are relevant criticisms, but it may not mean we throw out the thesis altogether.

First, a sufficiently complex piece of work — particularly one formed in multilayered medieval modes — can operate on a number of levels, and Lewis is sufficiently complex enough to work with character development and religious symbolism in concert with some other kind of shaping idea. By example, when Ransom's heel is wounded in his battle with the Unman at the close of *Perelandra*, there is no reason to choose whether this is a fulfillment of Genesis 3:15 or an Arthurian dolorous stroke.

---

[13] Lewis, *The Discarded Image*, 104.

In Lewis, the two are united by a common symbolic field of gravity. Lewis could, therefore, unite Christology and medieval cosmology with poetic themes.

Second, though I think the secrecy element in Lewis's life is overdrawn, and I have serious questions about how "kappa" is interpreted in the manuscript history of "On Stories,"[14] Ward is possibly correct that Lewis's personality was such that he would relish such a symmetrical plan and enjoy keeping it a secret.

Granted, then, that Lewis would for religious, ethical, or artistic reasons consider using a hidden construct, and that he was capable of it, the only possible way to evaluate the *Planet Narnia* thesis of book-to-planet correspondence is to decide if there is enough evidence in favour of it on internal grounds. Is there enough evidence of Martial influence in *Prince Caspian* or Saturnine influence in *The Last Battle*, and a lack of such guiding influence in the other books, to convince a skeptical reader that the construct is clear?

It is in this realm of criticism that the thesis fails. Because the Chronicles are so filled with planetary imagery, critically laid out so well, we can only accept that each book has its own guiding planetary intelligence by reducing that planetary influence in the other books.

"Jupiter, the King ... is Not Very Easy to Grasp" [15]

Most of us who picked up one of Ward's books were struck by the beautiful synchronicity between medieval cosmology and the Narniad. *The Lion, the Witch and the Wardrobe* is certainly a jovial book, just as *The Voyage of*

---

[14] See Ward, *Planet Narnia*, esp. 15-19.
[15] Lewis, *The Discarded Image*, 105.

the Dawn Treader is shot through with light and the Narnian civil war is the organizing principle of the martial *Prince Caspian*. The links are just very cool.

However, I have some concerns about Ward's selection of the qualities of the planets and the way they connect to the books. My biggest concern can be illustrated by looking at Ward's treatment of Jupiter in *That Hideous Strength*. He presses the argument that Jupiter is the guiding influence of *THS*. Ward's writing on the Ransom Cycle is thrilling to read, highlighting the planetary influence in a way that made me convinced I have undervalued the planets in thinking of THS as Thulcandra. However, Ward goes too far in making Jupiter/Jove the ruling influence of THS:

> The priestly-kingly operations of Jove manifest themselves in two main ways in *That Hideous Strength*: at a human level in the character of Ransom and at a cosmic level in the actual descent of Jupiter in chapter 15.[16]

Consider the details in that section: Ransom is the Pendragon, and thus King of Logres, but also a Christ figure; Melchisedec was the priest-king and Christ figure; Ransom is thus not just king but priest-king; "Melchisedec is a Hebrew name meaning 'My king is Jupiter'";[17] Ransom survives on a diet of wine and bread and has a jovial nature; therefore, Ransom is a jovial character and kingship comes to the front of *THS*.

---

[16] Ward, *Planet Narnia*, 49.
[17] Ibid., 50.

The link is thin; Ward has pressed the Melchisedec idea too far.[18] More than this though — and I would like to major on majors — does *THS* strike you as a jovial book dominated by the theme of kingship? It clearly isn't jovial, and Ransom himself downplays the kingship theme, noting that he is a subject of the impotent King of England, and we see nothing like the kingship material of most Arthurian tales. Merlin the king-maker is stripped of his role and Ransom must make him a new kind of mage.

If we were to press the question of which planetary influence we would want to identify with *That Hideous Strength*, what would it be? The book takes places during Saturnalia, and it is Saturnine kind of atmosphere. Note the atmosphere when Saturn (Lurga) descends upon the Manor at St. Anne's in chapter 15.

By contrast, *THS* is clearly about Venus. The book is bookended by the marriage ceremony, beginning in troth-making and ending in consummation. A critical theme concerns the various kinds of obediences and self-deaths that are played out in stories of romantic love. *THS* is a venereal book.

Looking at the title, we see that *That Hideous Strength* is a reference to a 16th century poem about the Tower of Babel. Clearly a major theme is language, making it a book about Hermes-Mercury-Viritrilbia, the planet where language is born. While Mark and Jane are caught in a Venus-tale, consider that Lewis in his poem "The Planets" described Mercury with these words:

---

[18] In reading for my two biblical degrees—including two years of Hebrew—Melchizedek was never connected with Jupiter. To most readers, "Melchizedek" means "king of righteousness" or "my king is righteous." It is true that Jews called Jupiter 'Tzedeq' (the same root). I am not certain we have any reference to Jupiter in the 2000 years of biblical history between Abraham and the Talmud, but I'm open to be corrected. Even if I am wrong, did Lewis, though, have any idea of this technical point of Hebrew? I am doubtful.

"Words in wedlock, and wedding also" — fitting for the mercurial journey they are on: apart, together, apart, together, like quicksilver in a dish.

Clearly Mercury, certainly Venus, obviously Saturn, and Jupiter are important. We fail in supposing that we have to choose one planetary theme. Ward concludes, "Clearly, Ransom has become a personification of Jupiter, and it is no surprise in the final chapter when we see him sitting 'crowned, at the right of the hearth.'"[19] That supremacy is not clear, and yet it is valuable to bring out the embedded themes of kingship and joviality lost in a saturnine text-world with a mercurial plot. Avoiding planetary reductionism, which is Ward's core limitation, and attending to the forty pages of *Planet Narnia* specifically concerned with the Ransom Cycle will make you a better reader of those overlooked books.

However, the pressing of Jupiter on this point might be telling. When you think of the book, is the theme of kingship really best shown in *The Lion, the Witch and the Wardrobe*? *Prince Caspian*, *The Silver Chair*, *The Voyage of the Dawn Treader*, and *The Horse and His Boy* are essentially about the nature of true kingship. In *Prince Caspian* Peter must surrender his leadership to Lucy's spiritual wisdom and Edmund's counsel in order to be a true king. Caspian in *The Voyage of the Dawn Treader* and Tirian in *The Last Battle* are both tested severely in their kingliness, and the very first king of Narnia is set up with the core teachings of kingship in *The Magician's Nephew*. Caspian X, Rilian, and Shasta are each lost kings who must find their way back to their proper place. The kingship

---

[19] Ward, *Planet Narnia*, 50.

theme is no more prevalent in *The Lion, the Witch and the Wardrobe* than elsewhere, and certainly less central than some (*The Horse and His Boy* and *Prince Caspian*).

Thinking of other Jupiter characteristics, *The Lion, the Witch and the Wardrobe* may be the most jovial book, but is it the most sanguine (or do sanguine characters predominate)? Is Aslan the most temperate in *The Lion, the Witch and the Wardrobe*? Is *The Lion, the Witch and the Wardrobe* the most festal, or would *Prince Caspian* not fill that role? Is the attention to lion-heartedness any greater in *The Lion, the Witch and the Wardrobe* than *The Silver Chair* or *The Voyage of the Dawn Treader*? I do not deny the striking connection between the Jupiter section of "The Planets" and the *The Lion, the Witch and the Wardrobe* plot, which is at the heart of Lewis's understanding of redemption.[20] I simply do not think that *The Lion, the Witch and the Wardrobe* is exclusively or even primarily about Jupiter, the greatest and kingliest of planets.

Challenging "The Martial Temperament"[21]

Another challenge I would offer is the way that Ward correlated Mars with Prince Caspian. Ward twins the martial god of war with Mars Silvanus. Historically, though, the Mars Silvanus influence is far less strong in both poetry and worship,[22] and Mars Silvanus is more of a farming god than a forest or merely verdant figure. The martial

---

[20] In telling his engaging story of discovery in lectures and interviews, Ward points to the striking note in Lewis's poem "The Planets" concerning Jupiter: "of winter passed / and guilt forgiven," C.S. Lewis, "The Alliterative Metre," in *Selected Literary Essays*, ed. Walter Hooper (Cambridge: Canto Classics, 2013); 26.

[21] Lewis, *The Discarded Image*, 106.

[22] Moreover, some attention to the ecosystems of parts of Europe might be helpful when thinking of agricultural gods when it comes to the spring language in *Planet Narnia*.

elements of Mars are no doubt key in the medieval world, though the historic Mars of worship is so widely described that almost any designation is possible when building a Mars character. Dangerous to Ward's thesis, Mars is a one-size-fits-all god.

Lewis, like Dante, partially undercuts the Mars image of god of war in *Out of the Silent Planet*. Though Lewis admired Holst's Mars movement, he knew his Malacandra had a different flavour, being a place of almost ultimate peace where violence looks like a scar in the text.[23] By contrast, the focus on Mars in Lewis's poem "The Planets" is entirely about fortune, help, and war — nothing vegetative or peaceful whatsoever.

Considering Mars in Narnia, even if we allow for trees and war as a twin image that Lewis could draw on, would we naturally turn to *Prince Caspian* for features of trees and war, or to *The Last Battle*?

Prince Caspian is indeed a book about the preparation for battle, though much of that preparation is hidden from description, as is much of the war. Of war in *Prince Caspian* we have mostly skirmishes and the hand-to-hand single challenge that establishes who is a true king of Narnia. *The Horse and His Boy* culminates in war with furious description, *The Lion, the Witch and the Wardrobe* climaxes on the battlefield, and the subtext of *The Silver Chair* is about an armed rebellion. Beyond these, *The Last Battle* is soaked with battle, beginning with a scene that brings the different Mars images together: the death of trees and the slaughter of the Dryads. Mars Silvanus and Mars Gradivus are united most specifically in

---

[23] Just as the past wars with the rebel Thulcandra scarred the Malacandran landscape.

The Last Battle as the first half of that book is about royal usurpation, enslavement, and martial decimation of the wood.

Mars, then, really is a double-edged sword: *The Horse and His Boy*, *The Last Battle*, and *Prince Caspian* are all books that play with that theme, but the first half of *The Last Battle* sits better as a martial-sylvan book with a saturnine atmosphere. And, of course, "battle" is in the title of *The Last Battle*. Ward uses that as evidence of Sol in *The Voyage of the Dawn Treader* and Luna in *The Silver Chair*, so the evidence is not insignificant.[24] Finally, think of this line from the Mars section of "The Planets": "with trees splintered / And birds banished."[25] This is like the cry of the Narnians in *The Last Battle*.

"The Celestial Dance"[26]

I have no doubt that Ward reads *The Voyage of the Dawn Treader* strongly as a "Sol" book, with light as a central theme.[27] *The Silver Chair* is the most lunatic book, but is it really the wettest (see *The Voyage of the Dawn Treader*'s voyage or the end-time flood in *The Last Battle*, a narrative filled with watery language) — and is wateriness really the dominant lunar theme in medieval poetry? Is *The Horse and His Boy* really the most language-soaked (hermetic) book, or should we look to the language play in *The Magician's Nephew* or the way that messages circulate as folklore in *The Lion, the Witch and the Wardrobe* or the fact that *The Silver Chair* is entirely structured around words? Saturn, especially when

---

[24] Silver being the metal of Luna.
[25] Lewis, "Alliterative Metre," 25.
[26] Lewis, *The Discarded Image*, 55.
[27] Though I believe it to be honestly informed by the "light" theme in John.

imaged as Father Time, fits better with the thematic currents of *The Silver Chair* better than *The Last Battle*. Though the saturnal, sickly, aged, weary nature of the Narnian world as *The Last Battle* begins is worth highlighting, could we speak of Father Time as pouring out a "perilous draught / That the lip loves not"?[28] Maybe, but the link is not obvious.

Most of all, describing *The Magician's Nephew* as a venereal book takes a great deal of imaginative energy. The Venus analysis sits poorly in *The Magician's Nephew*, though it might fit well with *The Voyage of the Dawn Treader*, which has "friendship" as a critical theme.[29] The Dawn Treader's voyage also fits Lewis's description of Venus in "The Planets" — "her secret sceptre, in the sea's caverns."[30]

"In Going Beyond the Contour Lines"[31]

All of these questions, queries, and critiques are meant to cause doubt that we should squeeze the seven planets into the form of seven books. Ward is correct that the Narniad is filled with planetary imagery, subtle, obvious, and interwoven in the text, story, characters, themes, and images. This intertextual layering is spiritually rich and imaginatively evocative. By pressing each planet into the frame of each book, however, Ward compresses the texts — the text of the medieval model and the text of Narnia — beyond what they can bear.

---

[28] Lewis, "Alliterative Metre," 26.
[29] Translating erotic love to friendship in a children's story.
[30] Ibid., 24.
[31] Lewis, *The Discarded Image*, 217.

Lewis believed that the planets needed "to be lived with imaginatively, not merely learned as concepts."[32] Lewis himself thought that the planets needed one another to work in tension, as Ward admits when he sees *The Last Battle* moving from the realm of Saturn to the realm of Jove. If we allow, then, for Ward's work to flow into the entire series, we see how the seven planets fill Lewis's imagination, and Lewis reaches back to the model as his word-hoard and his symbol-purse.

Prince Caspian is a martial book, but looking at the ways that the sword and the leaf come together throughout the Narniad is far truer to Mars intertextual realities — and is a reading rich in possibility. As the feast of Saturnalia is Dec. 21-23, just before Christmas, there is a benefit to regarding Narnia in *The Lion, the Witch and the Wardrobe* as under the influence of Saturn until that realm — "the Sun's finger / Daunted with darkness,"[33] as Lewis says of Saturn in "The Planets" — is broken by the self-sacrificial king. The sacrifice made, Venusian spring and Jovial lordship bursts upon the land.[34] The Witch's camp, then, turns to the support of Mars on the battlefield. After all, "Of evil and good. All's one to Mars,"[35] Lewis says, so her claim is as valid to the haughty mercenary god as any other. It turns out that the Witch is mistaken to trust Mars's "graceless beauty" and his "Blond insolence."[36] As a result, though Jadis hopes that she can become "the liar made lord," Aslan's self-sacrifice overcomes Mars's "iron."

---

[32] Lewis, *The Discarded Image*, 173.

[33] Lewis, "Alliterative Metre," 26.

[34] Of Venus: "In grass growing, and grain bursting, / Flower unfolding, and flesh longing, / And shower falling sharp in April," Lewis, "Alliterative Metre," 24.

[35] Ibid., 25.

[36] Ibid.

Frankly, allowing all the seven planets to poetically permeate *The Lion, the Witch and the Wardrobe* makes for suggestive readings that deepen Lewis's inversive message of honour, courage, integrity, loyalty, and self-sacrificial love. Extending Ward's research to an assessment of the Narniad as a whole and the meaning of *The Chronicles* deepens it even further.

My critical questions and brief experiments suggest procrustean limitations to Ward's thesis as it stands, but limitless possibilities for readers who use *Planet Narnia* as a resource for further work.

"After Considering All the Evidence Afresh"[37]

Broken into parts, Michael Ward's thesis is that:

1. Lewis was imaginatively invested in medieval planetary imagery;
2. Therefore, that imagery informs Narnia;
3. Lewis intentionally shaped the Narniad by the seven planetary influences;
4. By aligning each Narnian chronicle with a particular medieval planet;
5. And hid his structure from friends and readers.

In literary criticism we can rarely speak with absolute certainty and so must discuss things in terms of relative degrees of probability. With historical and biographical criticism — despite Lewis's resistance to those disciplines — Michael Ward has established point #1 with near certainty. *Planet Narnia* establishes point #2 as highly probable and the reader can easily test this part of the

---

[37] Lewis, *The Discarded Image*, 180.

thesis. Point #5 is non-falsifiable, so we cannot assess its probability or agree to it in an evidence-based way. Point #4 I have attempted to put into doubt, but to do so in a way that confirms the first two points.

Which leaves us with point #3, the question of intentionality. To what degree did Lewis intentionally infuse Narnia with planetary images (whether Ward is right or whether my cautions are valid)? The answer is that we cannot know without external text evidence. You may say that the sheer number of planetary and cosmological references is overwhelming, so Lewis must have been aware of what he was doing. I actually agree and would say that point #3 is highly probable (though not with relation to point #4). But we must admit that we don't have a method for saying how many references account for accidental intertextuality and how many constitute proof of intention.

Of course, we don't need to know point #3 to affirm the best part of the *Planet Narnia* thesis. Intriguingly, if we leave #3 aside, Ward's point #4 no longer needs the problematic secrecy theory, point #5. Focusing on the text and the world of the text — as Lewis asks us to do in reading — allows us all the benefits of the thesis without the deeply implausible and untestable occultation thesis.

And, of course, this is true even if Ward's most intriguing claim — point #4, that the Narniad is structured according to the sevenfold planetary model — is demonstrably true. My negation of Ward's secrecy theory is not disastrous to his thesis as a whole. We don't need to create a fiction about Lewis's writing process to consider the *Planet Narnia* thesis. Lewis has given us the text and we should read it.[38]

Though I reject the hot points of Ward's thesis, I think it is a stellar work as a whole. This is why I offer my inadequate response here. I hope that readers can use the book to strengthen their experience of Narnia and, in a complementary way, strengthen their attention to method, logic, and analysis in scholarship.

---

[38] Which is Lewis's primary argument in his first and last works of literary theory. C.S. Lewis and E.M.W. Tillyard, *The Personal Heresy: A Controversy* (New York: HarperOne, 1939); C.S. Lewis, *An Experiment in Criticism* (Cambridge: Canto Classics, 2012).

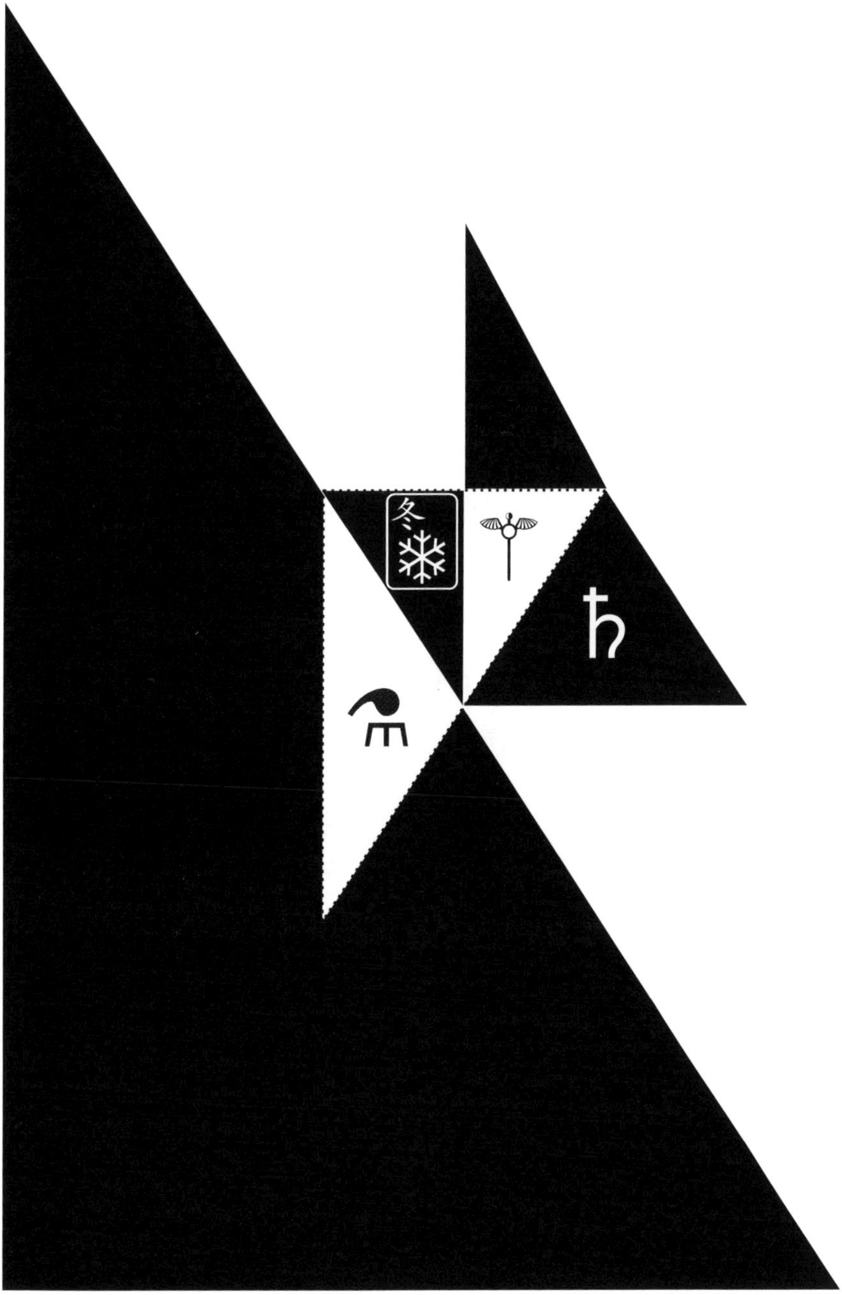
冬

$$P(h|e\&k) = \frac{P(e|h\&k)P(h|k)}{P(e|k)}$$

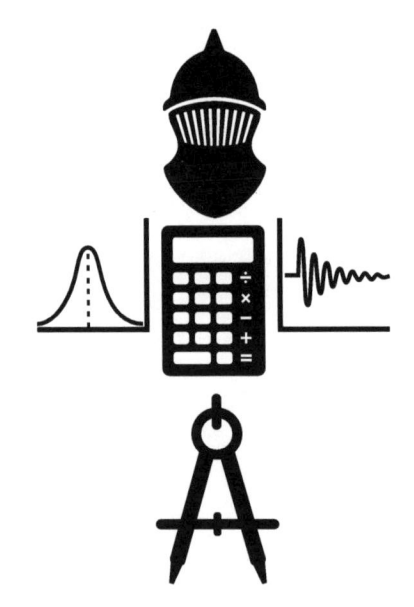

A Defense of Planet Narnia

Josiah Peterson

You may be surprised, as I was, to learn that Michael Ward's *Planet Narnia* thesis is controversial. You may, like me, have needed little "proof" beyond the Jove stanza of the "The Planets" poem ("of winter passed / And guilt forgiven," "The lion-hearted," "Just and gentle, are Jove's children," etc.) and a brief sketch of the various planetary associations Lewis makes in *The Discarded Image* from which you were easily able to make the connections with the corresponding books. Reading or watching *The Narnia Code* or *Planet Narnia* only confirmed what you already believed was probably true. But other scholars — among them some very serious and respected Lewis scholars — are not so easily satisfied. They raise several objections to the thesis with varying degrees of severity. This paper aims to categorize and summarize the objections made to Ward's *Planet Narnia* thesis, sketch out responses to the objections, and propose a theoretical framework to better evaluate the thesis.

Ward's thesis can be briefly summarized as follows: "the Narnia stories were designed to express the characteristics of the seven medieval planets — Jupiter, Mars, Sol, Luna, Mercury, Venus, and Saturn. Lewis constructed the Chronicles so that in each book the plot-line, the ornamental details, and the portrayal of the

Christ-figure of Aslan, all serve to communicate the governing planetary personality."[1]

The objections to Ward's thesis can be broken down into two broad categories: *de jure* objections which hold that a thesis like Ward's is simply out of court to begin with, and *de facto* objections which hold that Ward's thesis, while possible, is not born out by the facts of the books themselves.

De Jure Critique

Rejection of the "Code" Language

Some critics, such as Devin Brown or James Como, object to the *Planet Narnia* thesis on the basis that the Narniad does not require a code and that the suggestion of a code implies that Lewis's work is somehow insufficient without it.[2] A 'code' — by their thinking — would mean that either the books cannot be properly appreciated without knowledge of the code or that the literary quality of the books itself depends on the existence of an interpretive key. As devotees of Lewis, they reject either possibility and are particularly bothered by Ward's invocation of the "problem of composition" in the introductory chapter of *Planet Narnia*, in which Ward lists off a number of critics who believe the Narnia books lack a unifying theme or coherent structure.[3] Ward's critics think he gives too much credit to Lewis's critics.

---

[1] Michael Ward, *Planet Narnia: The Seven Heavens in the Imagination of C.S. Lewis* (New York: Oxford University Press, 2010), back cover. For a fuller exploration of Ward's argument, see also *The Narnia Code: C.S. Lewis and the Secret of the Seven Heavens*, or visit www.planetnarnia.com/planet-narnia.

[2] Devin Brown, "Planet Narnia Spin, Spun Out," CSLewis.com, May 13, 2009.

[3] Ward, *Planet Narnia: The Seven Heavens in the Imagination of C.S. Lewis* (New York: Oxford, 2008), 8-14.

Falsifiability

Other critics have held that Ward's thesis is too *ad hoc* to be rigorously tested or applied. They believe Ward cherry picks his evidence — taking the battles from *Prince Caspian* as evidence of Mars's influence while dismissing the scene of Aslan staring up at the moon or taking the verdant garden in *Magician's Nephew* to indicate Venus while downplaying Digory's vision of Jupiter as he descends through the world pool. It troubles his critics when Ward begins quoting Lewis, saying "all the planets are represented in each," or "in a certain juncture of the planets each may play the other's part," or that the gods "flow in and out of one another like eddies on a river."[4] If it is all nebulous, the thesis cannot be worth all that much as a key to understanding the Chronicles.

Lewis and the Artistic Method

Some critics, including Brown, reject the notion that Lewis, when crafting a particular scene, would limit himself to structures that evoke the correct planetary imagery, rather than availing himself of anything that makes for the best scene possible. According to them, that is simply not how writers write. Additionally, they point to the fact that Lewis describes his own writing process as being spurred by recurring images of lions, queens in sledges, and fauns under lamp posts. This planetary theme doesn't square with the creative process that would be required if Ward's thesis is true.

Why Would Lewis Hide It?

A common critique regarding Ward's thesis is this: If Lewis was engaged in the grand project of embedding medieval planetary imagery and atmosphere into all of his stories, what reason could he have to hide it from the public, let alone his closest friends and even his own stepson?

---

[4] Ward, *Planet Narnia*. 226, 212, 232.

The "So What?" Objection

Some who hear Dr. Ward's thesis respond with what they believe to be the damning question, "So what?" If a thesis is true, it ought to really change the way we see and appreciate something. It ought to be revolutionary. If we follow the thesis and not much changes about how we read the books, then it must not be true.

De Facto Critique

The Bean Counter

Justin Barrett made a serious attempt to quantifiably test Dr. Ward's thesis.[5] How could we test such a thesis quantitatively? He suggests tabulating every word Ward mentions as associated with each of the planetary influences and then statistically analyzing how frequently each of those words appears in each of the seven books. Barrett certainly did his due diligence in compiling his data. He accommodated the page length of each of the books into his frequencies, and also ran the test both with the absolute frequencies of word references, and the relative frequencies of particular words — for example, does a given book have a higher frequency of the collective total of jovial words, and does a book have higher frequencies of specific jovial words? He found that there are strong correlations between the planetary words with the books Ward's thesis predicts in four out of the seven books, and a weak correlation for a fifth book, *Prince Caspian*. He found the correlations did not align for *The Lion, the Witch and the Wardrobe* with Jove and *The Last Battle* with Saturn.

---

[5] Justin Barrett, "Some Planets in Narnia: A Quantitative Investigation of the Planet Narnia Thesis," *VII* 27 (January 2010), accessed December 3, 2018, https://www.wheaton.edu/media/migrated-images-amp-files/media/files/centers-and-institutes/wade-center/Barrett_Narnia_web.pdf.

The "Planets Everywhere!" Critique

A less precise but possibly more compelling criticism is that the planetary influences are not sufficiently distinct in each of the books. How is it that *The Lion, the Witch and the Wardrobe* is the jovial book and *Prince Caspian* the martial book when Peter and Edmund are knighted after their battles in the former and the latter is all about establishing the true king of Narnia and ends with a bacchanalia? What about the dozen references to the moon in *The Horse and his Boy* and the presence of Father Time (i.e. Saturn) in the caves of the underworld in *The Silver Chair*? Critics with this view may greatly appreciate Ward's exploration of the presence of medieval cosmology in Lewis's work but reject the 'strong' version of Ward's thesis that would assign a planet to each book.

Responses

The first thing to note in responding to the criticisms is that neither the 'code' critique nor the 'so what?' critique are sufficient defeaters for Ward's thesis. It is entirely possible to reject the "problem of composition" — that is, to believe the books are perfectly fine as a set without Ward's thesis to bind them together — while still holding that Lewis worked in the seven planetary themes into the seven books. The rooms of a house may be functionally laid out in relation to one another *and* in relation to the particular views of the landscape outside their windows. Far from slighting Lewis's genius, Ward's thesis, if true, marks Lewis out to be an even greater and more subtle literary craftsman than previously thought.

Additional responses are required for the "so what?" critique. One is tempted to respond that the failure to find significance in the thesis lies with the deficient imaginations of the critics rather than with the thesis, but this would be ungenerous and not in keeping with the nuance of Ward's argument. Not everyone who is familiar with Ward's thesis will enjoy the reading more because of it. If Ward is right about Lewis's imagery and the theme of the medieval cosmology, then the thesis idea has been a possible influence in the reader's enjoyment of the books. The *Planet Narnia* thesis is not primarily geared toward enhancing our *enjoyment* of the books; however, it offers us a framework to *contemplate* the the source of our enjoyment. It is like when a layman is moved by a particular piece of visual art and an art major comes along and explains the various methods used to produce the effects the viewer is experiencing. The art major's explanation may have little effect on the layman's enjoyment of the piece of art, but that does not mean the art major is wrong in their assessment of the artistic method employed.

Understanding the possible symbolism and meaning in the story may not produce any significant or new enjoyment of the texts — it may even lessen it if we turn all our attention to it — but it may help us better appreciate the genius of the author. While valuing the author *as an author* is far from the goal of enjoying a good book, it is not a bad practice in which to engage if one is trying to better appreciate the craft of writing.

The 'artistic' critique might be more destructive if it were not so poorly developed to begin with. In his article "Planet Narnia Spin, Spun Out," Devin Brown quotes the *Planet Narnia* website where Ward asks, "Why does the Christ-like figure of Aslan enter the story among dancing trees in *Prince Caspian*? Why does he fly in a sunbeam in *The Voyage of the Dawn Treader*? Why is he mistaken for two lions in *The Horse and His Boy*? Why does he not appear in Narnia at all in *The Silver Chair*?"[6] Ward's implied answer is that in each of these scenes, Lewis is surrounding Aslan's presence (or absence) with elements reminiscent of the planet in whose character each book is written. In response Brown writes, "Dr. Ward would have us believe that on each of these occasions, Lewis did not simply ask what would be the best element for the story but instead asked, 'What can I do here that will fit with this book's planet?'"[7] But of course this is a false dichotomy. If Ward's thesis is true, then what best fits with the book's planet *is* what would be the best element for the story.

As to why Lewis never mentions the planets as part of his method, Ward's thesis is that Lewis hoped the planetary imagery and themes would be appealing to the readers at a deeper, experiential level rather than a conscious level. Lewis was not as concerned with our propositional thinking about medieval cosmology as he was with our psychological, even spiritual, reactions to it. The reader's reactions to the planetary images and themes would come independently of their knowledge of the medieval sources behind them, and would perhaps come through more easily without the distraction or impediment of being aware of what Lewis is attempting.[8] One may still find the total secrecy to be a weak point in the overall thesis, but given Ward's plausible explanations for Lewis's desire to keep his project under wraps, any doubts on this

---

[6] Michael Ward, "Planet Narnia," *PlanetNarnia.com*, accessed November 20, 2018. http://www.planetnarnia.com/planet-narnia.

[7] Devin Brown, "Planet Narnia Spin, Spun Out," *CSLewis.com*, May 13, 2009. http://www.cslewis.com/planet-narnia-spin-spun-out/.

[8] Think of how much profound moral philosophy Lewis was able to get through to his secular and morally skeptical audience under the unassuming guise of "Reflections on education with special reference to the teaching of English in the upper forms of schools." Lewis was not beneath the tactic of employing misdirection to get through to his audience.

ground ought to be weighed against the evidence presented for the thesis as a whole. This, of course, raises the question of how to go about evaluating the evidence.

'Falsifiability' and the 'planets everywhere' critiques can all be answered with a more rigorous criterion for evaluating the thesis. For all of Barrett's fascinating research, the numerical approach ultimately proves inadequate on several levels. First, one hardly knows what to do with a 71.4% approval rating produced by such a method. The data does not interpret itself. Is a 71.4% a passing rate or ought it to be higher? Second, as Ward points out in his response to Barrett in his aptly titled "Quality not Quantity," Barrett's method of counting words cannot possibly capture the significance of the words in the context and the overall story. Ward states, "I trust him when he reports that the words "death" and "dying" appear as many times in *The Silver Chair* as they do in *The Last Battle*. But how many characters actually die in *The Silver Chair*?"[9] Additionally, in order for Lewis's writing to trigger Barrett's test, he would have to write in a rather overt, even grossly obvious manner, which would be antithetical to having the planets operating as the subtle influence pervading the stories.[10] Finally, I think Barrett's efforts can easily be put to rest when we observe that, according to his method, *The Silver Chair* would garner the label of the most jovial book while *The Last Battle* fails to be most saturnine.[11] These two results — obviously

---

[9] Michael Ward, "Quality not Quantity," *VII* Vol 28 (2012), accessed December 3, 2018, https://www.wheaton.edu/media/migrated-images-amp-files/media/files/centers-and-institutes/wade-center/vii/vii20online20articles/Ward_QualityorQuantity2.pdf.

[10] Ibid., 7.

[11] Barrett, 6.

absurd to anyone who has read either book — on their own are sufficient to undermine his methodology.

Bayes' Theorem

Without proposing the introduction of any actual numbers or probabilities, I propose Bayes' Theorem as a theoretical framework for evaluating Ward's thesis. Bayes looks at the relationship between three elements: an hypothesis (h), evidence (e), and background knowledge (k) to assess the probability (P) of the hypothesis. Bayes asks whether or not we should expect the evidence we have, given the hypothesis [$P(e|h\&k)$] (i.e., the explanatory power of the hypothesis), and how it compares to the prior probability of the hypothesis [$P(h|k)$] (i.e. was the hypothesis likely to be true given the rest of what we know), and the prior probability of the evidence [$P(e|k)$] (i.e., to what extent did the evidence require an explanation). The resulting formulation is:

$$P(h|e\&k) = \frac{P(e|h\&k)P(h|k)}{P(e|k)}$$

But the formula is less important than the concepts. Does the hypothesis explain the evidence? Did the evidence need explaining? Is the hypothesis independent and likely, given what else we know? All of the criticisms of Ward's thesis can be fit into the Bayesian model.

The explanatory power of Ward's thesis is quite strong. Apart from the mode of Aslan's appearances described above, there are the prevailing thematic conflicts of the books: the austere queen versus the magnanimous king in *Lion*; the Machiavellian tyrant versus the gallant resistance in *Caspian*; the constant revealing and testing of the protagonists in *Dawn Treader* versus the obfuscating officials and the literally dark island; and the competing dreams and visions and questionable sanity at play in *Silver Chair*; the perpetual joining and separating on a flight home in *A Horse and his Boy*; the genocidal tyrant of a dying world versus the gentle monarch bringing life to a new world in *The Magician's Nephew*; and the confounding of all plans and end of the world in *Last Battle*. Then there are particular pieces of evidence: the Narnian Lord with a winged helmet in *A Horse and his Boy*, the similarity between Castor — the horse-riding twin to the boxer Pollux in Mercury's constellation, Gemini — to the protagonist Shasta whose real name we learn is Cor and who is a horse-riding twin with a brother who's always boxing.[12] These are what we should expect to see if Ward's thesis were true. Of course, this is also where contradictory evidence, both general and particular, must also be evaluated.

The explanatory power of the thesis must be evaluated in light of the prior probability of the evidence existing in spite of the thesis. It is on this ground that "Code" critics can argue that Father Christmas has a legitimate place in Narnia without the need for a jovial planetary framework. This is also where "Planets Everywhere" critics argue that we should expect plenty of planetary imagery in Narnia even if Lewis were not writing the books to conform to particular planetary virtues. But can either account for the winged helmet and the similarity between Shasta/Cor and Castor mentioned above? We can also ask whether it was possible or

---

[12] Ward, *Planet Narnia*, 153.

desirable to write a book with unique elements of a single planet to the complete exclusion of all others.

Finally, one must consider the prior probability of the hypothesis — namely, how likely it would be that Lewis would employ such a method of writing and conceal it from everyone. These questions are the subject of the first two chapters of *Planet Narnia*. Honest critics, I believe, must be persuaded that Lewis could and would employ such a method given his stated interests in rehabilitating the medieval model of the universe and his particular theories about how we appreciate stories. So the real conflict lies in the question of secrecy, addressed above in the response to artistic method. My own final assessment is that the explanatory power of the evidence $[P(e|h \& k)]$ is fairly high, that the prior probability of the cumulative evidence $[P(e|k)]$ is low, and that the prior probability of the hypothesis $[P(h|k)]$ is high enough for the whole thesis to be more than likely true. You may conclude otherwise, but before you do so, I hope that you first consider the analytical tools offered here.

Ana- { **MARY / ARMY** } *gram.*

How well her name an *Army* doth present,
In whom the *Lord of Hosts* did pitch his tent!

— George Herbert
from *The Temple*, 1633

Return to Planet Narnia

Michael Ward

> How well her name an *Army* doth present,
> In whom the *Lord of Hosts* did pitch his tent!
> — Ana- {Mary/Army} gram, George Herbert

> "To arms! To arms, Telmar!" . . . "To arms, Narnia!"
> — Prince Caspian, C.S. Lewis

When talking about the discovery of an interpretative key for a novel, C.S. Lewis observes that the only way to test the supposed key would be to repeatedly re-read the novel in its light and see how well it illuminated the work. If the key were genuine, Lewis says, "then at every fresh . . . reading of the book, we should find it settling down, making itself more at home, and eliciting significance from all sorts of details in the whole work which we had hitherto neglected."[1] As I have freshly read and re-read Lewis's Chronicles of Narnia in the light of the interpretative key provided by the seven heavens, the more they have yielded up their secrets and unveiled the intelligence and skill which went into their composition. In this essay, I will

---

[1] C.S. Lewis, *Miracles: A Preliminary Study* (Glasgow: Collins, 1980), 113.

present several new pieces of evidence in support of my contention that the second Chronicle, *Prince Caspian: The Return to Narnia*, embodies and expresses the personality of the planet, Mars.

I should make it clear that I am not attempting here any substantial argument, but only further illustrations in support of the argument developed at length in *Planet Narnia* and in particular in its fourth chapter. If readers have not already been persuaded of the Narniad's planetary design, and of the martial donegality of *Prince Caspian*, they are unlikely to find the following essay convincing. I suspect that the details enumerated here may seem inconsequential in isolation from the parent book, as ineffective and unattractive as coals removed from the fire in the grate. However, I dare to assume there will be some readers familiar with and sufficiently persuaded by the case propounded in *Planet Narnia*; it is for them that I write.

Though Lewis's knowledge of medieval literature can sometimes seem so vast as to be comprehensive, even Homer nods, and Lewis's expertise had its limits. In *Planet Narnia*, I quoted a rare confession of ignorance on his part. Commenting upon Chaucer's *Compleynt of Mars*, Lewis said that "the astronomical allusions are, I confess, too hard for me." I went on to confess the fact that some of the Martial connections of his own *Prince Caspian* were likewise too hard for me, acknowledging that I could not explain the Mars-related significance of the name of the eponymous hero, Caspian.[2]

---

[2] Michael Ward, *Planet Narnia* (Oxford: Oxford University Press, 2008), 274 n44.

Thanks to the draft of the poem "The Planets" that Lewis scholar Charlie Starr has helpfully brought to my attention, I now think it is possible to give a reason for Lewis's choice of the name "Caspian" because, in that draft, Lewis describes the heaven of Mars as "the sky's Scythia."[3] Here are the relevant lines:

> . . . But other country,
> Dark with discord, dins beyond him [Sol],
> With noise of nakers and neighing horses,
> The sky's Scythia. A scornful god,
> MARS mercenary, makes his camp there,
> And flies his flag . . .

According to the ancient Greek historian Herodotus (whose work Lewis, as an Oxford-educated classicist, knew intimately), the Scythians — the tribe of people prominent in Eurasia from about the ninth till the first century before Christ — had a peculiar devotion to the god Mars.[4] They were among the first peoples to master mounted warfare and appear to have had a reputation for being especially barbaric (which helps explain, by the way, St Paul's statement in his Letter to the Colossians that "Here there is no . . . barbarian, Scythian, slave or free").[5] It was only in the cult of Mars that the Scythians used images, altars, and temples; the rites they paid to Mars were unique, and they made more sacrifices to Mars "than to all the rest of the gods."[6]

---

[3] This draft is found in a notebook now in the possession of Walter Hooper. In this notebook, Lewis fair copied a number of his poems from the years circa 1929-1938. Included among these handwritten poems is a version of "The Planets" (numbered 'XXVIII'), which Starr estimates was copied in around 1935, i.e., shortly before or shortly after the publication of the poem in the magazine *Lysistrata* (Vol. II, No. I, May 1935), 21-24.

[4] See, e.g., his parody, "A Lost Chapter of Herodotus."

[5] Col. 3:11.

[6] Herodotus, *The Histories*, book IV.

With these facts in mind we can better understand Lewis's description in "The Planets" of the sphere of Mars as "the sky's Scythia," for the Martial heaven would naturally be attractive to the Scythians. But it may also explain why Lewis chose to name his protagonist 'Caspian' because the realm of Scythia consisted of the Pontic-Caspian steppe, the plains that stretch from the north coast of the Black Sea all the way east to the Caspian Sea.

Though this geographical link may — at least, partially — explain the choice of the name of the eponymous hero, we must ask a further question: of all the places within the borders of Scythia that might have supplied Lewis with a name for his protagonist, what was it about the word 'Caspian' that particularly caught his attention?

One possibility is that Lewis has in mind the Caspian Pass, which, according to Pliny was a very narrow defile in the Caspian mountains.[7] It is perhaps at Pliny that Lewis is glancing in his description of the almost invisible "steep and narrow path going slant-wise down into the gorge between rocks" through which Aslan guides the children at a critical juncture in the tale.[8]

Another possibility is etymological. 'Caspian', like the term 'Caucasian', was originally a native self-designation, meaning 'white' by extension from 'snow' or 'ice'.[9] On the face of it, whiteness would hardly seem appropriate for the hero of a Martial tale, for whiteness often suggests fear or even cowardice. Hence, "tough-looking warriors turned

---

[7] Herodotus, *The Histories*, VI.17.
[8] C.S. Lewis, *Prince Caspian* (New York: HarperCollins, 2001) 384.
[9] Pliny the Elder in his *Natural History* (Book 6, ch. 17) derives 'Caucasus' from the Scythian term 'Croucasis', meaning 'white with snow'. See the translation by W.H.S. Jones in the 10-volume edition of the *Natural History* (Cambridge, MA: Harvard University Press, 1949-54).

white" when the Awakened Trees came hurtling towards them.[10] Lewis as a young man during the Great War would perhaps have known personally, or at least have heard about, certain male contemporaries of his who, for refusing to serve in the armed forces, would have been "given the white feather," to signify their supposed cowardice. Such feathers were literally attached to the clothing or sent to the homes of able-bodied young men who decided not to sign up. The intention, of course, was to shame them into action.

But the hero of a Martial tale can hardly be a coward, so what might be the reason for Lewis's protagonist bearing a name that means 'white'? There are at least two possible explanations.

The first is that, according to "The Planets," "white-feathered dread / Mars has mastered." Given the meaning of 'Caspian', it appears that Lewis chose this name for the hero of his story in order to denote a character whose chivalric spirit is so pure, so perfectly 'hardened' by Martial influence,[11] one who has so completely mastered dread, that he has nothing to fear even from bearing a name, white, that would otherwise be suggestive of timidity or pusillanimity.[12]

---

[10] Lewis, *Prince Caspian*, 406.

[11] Mars produces "sturdy hardiness" (The Discarded Image, 106); "the hard virtue of Mars" ("The Adam at Night," Poems, 59). Accordingly, Caspian begins "to harden" as he sleeps "under the stars" (ch. 7).

[12] "Fear Him, ye saints, and you will then / Have nothing else to fear." Lewis described this line from the hymn "Through all the changing scenes of life" as "perfection." See C.S. Lewis, *Image and Imagination* (Cambridge: Cambridge University Press, 2013), 164.

The second explanation has to do with conventional portrayals of knighthood in medieval literature. We know that Lewis had a great love for Chaucer's "Knight's Tale," and so it is worth noting that the victor in that story, Palamon, who is attended by white bulls and white wolfhounds,[13] comes to the combat "with baner whyt and hardy chiere and face."[14] Lewis was also fully familiar with Malory's Arthurian legends in which a mysterious "white knight," dressed "in white armour, horse and all," bestows the shield "white as any snow" upon Sir Galahad, while he sojourns at a "white abbey."[15] It is to these sources, and others besides, that Lewis is respectfully, albeit obliquely, nodding when he selects 'Caspian' as the name for his hero in this tale. Prince Caspian, or 'Prince White' as we might legitimately call him, who is the first to receive the "Knighthood of the Order of the Lion"[16] at the end of the story, is part of a long line of "verray parfit gentil"[17] knights throughout literary history. Yet, rather than make his protagonist's moral purity too obvious, Lewis shields it behind a Scythian name which, once we cotton on to it, simultaneously strengthens the Martial theme.

While Caspian may represent the ideal kind of Scythian, what of his foes? Here again we will learn

---

[13] See "The Knight's Tale," lines 2139 and 2148.

[14] "With a white banner and with a hardy spirit and appearance" (line 2586). Interestingly, Palamon prays to Venus, whereas his opponent, Arcite, prays to Mars. Chaucer gives victory to the knight who fights under the goddess of love, not the knight who fights under the god of might. Lewis appeared to approve of balancing things out in this fashion; hence the final chapter of *That Hideous Strength* features "Venus at St Anne's," not Mars. For more on the victory of love over war, see *Planet Narnia*, 87.

[15] *Le Morte Darthur*, Sir Thomas Malory (Oxford: Oxford University Press, 1998), 321-322. For Lewis's scholarship in this field, see his essay "The 'Morte Darthur'" in *Studies in Medieval and Renaissance Literature*, ed. Walter Hooper (Cambridge: Cambridge University Press, 1966), 103-110. Lewis's boyhood nickname for this friend, Arthur Greeves, was 'Galahad' (see letter of 11 May 1915).

[16] *Prince Caspian* is the only Chronicle in which the word 'knighthood' appears.

[17] *The Canterbury Tales, General Prologue*, Geoffrey Chaucer (line 72).

something by paying attention to the draft of "The Planets" poem, in which we read of "white-livered fear," rather than the "white-feathered dread" that made it into the published version. In referencing the liver, Lewis is drawing on the tradition of medieval thought that assigned virtues to certain bodily organs. The liver was believed to be the seat of courage, and a truly Martial liver would give warriors "stomach," as Shakespeare's Henry V puts it ("he which hath no stomach to this fight, / Let him depart").[18] It should come as no surprise, then, that the only time in all seven books of the Narniad where the liver is ever mentioned is in *Prince Caspian* when the cowardly Miraz, fretting over his "martial policy,"[19] scorns his courtiers for being "lily-livered."[20] The Telmarines' whiteness is not the whiteness that comes from having mastered dread through candour of heart, as Caspian has done, but from being morally anaemic, insufficiently hardened by the iron of Mars.

Having tackled the name of the protagonist, let us try and solve the mystery of the antagonist, Miraz, whose name is appropriately ambiguous for a man of very dubious character.

"Miraz" may in part come from "Almirazgual," the Moorish name for the constellation Perseus, meaning "Bearer of the Demon's Head." A similar sort of possibility is that it comes via the Spanish *almirez*, from the Arabic *al-*

---

[18] Shakespeare, *Henry V*. 4.3.35-36

[19] The word 'martial' appears twice and the word 'marshal' appears seven times in *Prince Caspian*; neither word appears even once in any of the other Chronicles. The word 'arms' occurs more often in this Mars story than in any other Narnian tale.

[20] Lewis, *Prince Caspian*, 401.

mihras, meaning a small portable metal mortar.[21] A mortar suggests the military might of the Telmarines, who now rule Narnia and who are sufficiently violent and dominant that the Old Narnians ("The People That Lived In Hiding") dare not show their face.[22] Either one of these meanings would be appropriate for the military officer who has killed his brother, usurped the throne, and now oversees the Telmarine forces that occupy Narnia and subjugate its folk.

On the other hand, everything else we see of Miraz and the Telmarines indicates that they are far from truly Martial. They are "afraid of the woods," wear unimpressive armour (see below), are awed by a boy herald (Edmund), and their supposedly "great lords," Glozelle and Sopespian, are not only ill-disciplined and perfidious, they have a dandified air like the French court in Henry V, asking "What's to do? An Attack?" while "strolling along their lines and picking their teeth after breakfast."[23]

Glozelle himself knows that Miraz has no self-confidence and so he cleverly plays on the king's fears of being thought a coward in order to arm-twist him into facing Peter in single combat. Glozelle, with Sopespian's connivance, advertises Edmund as a "young warrior," "in the flower of his youth," and "a very dangerous knight" and advises Miraz to avoid him and his big brother:

> "For though I have never been called a coward [said Glozelle], I must plainly say that to meet that young man in battle is more than my heart would serve me for. And if (as is likely) his brother, the High King, is

---

[21] See *A Comprehensive Etymological Dictionary of the Spanish Language with Families of Words Based on Indo-European Roots*, Vol. I (A-G), ed. Edward A. Roberts (Bloomington, IN: XLibris, 2014), 96.
[22] Lewis, *Prince Caspian*, 349.
[23] Ibid., 398.

> more dangerous than he—why, on your life, my Lord King, have nothing to do with him."
>
> "Plague on you!" cried Miraz. "It was not that sort of council I wanted. Do you think I am asking you if I should be afraid to meet this Peter (if there is such a man)? Do you think I fear him? . . . Are you trying to make it appear that I am as great a coward as your Lordship? ... You talk like an old woman ... Are you soldiers? Are you Telmarines? Are you men? And if I do refuse it (as all good reasons of captaincy and martial policy urge me to do) you will think, and teach others to think, I was afraid. Is it not so? ... With your womanish counsels (ever shying from the true point, which is one of policy) you have done the very opposite of your intent. I had meant to refuse it. But I'll accept it. Do you hear, accept it!" [24]

Miraz's desire to be thought a man and not the slightest bit effeminate helps explain the other implication of his name, for 'mortar' does not just mean an armoured explosive shell. It also means "an instrument for pounding or crushing," as in a pestle and mortar, the mortar being the cup or bowl in which the pestle pounds and grinds.[25] The sexual innuendo need not be explained: it has a long-standing lineage in English literature — most famously, of course, in Beaumont's play, *The Knight of the Burning Pestle*.[26] For a knight to be associated with a pestle would bespeak his manliness; for him to be associated with a mortar is the very last thing he would want. In this respect, Miraz's name reveals that he is not truly knightly, not properly receptive to the Martial influence, as indeed is suggested even by the sound of his name, 'Miraz' being a garbled imitation of 'Mars'.

---

[24] Lewis, *Prince Caspian*, 400.

[25] Indeed, 'mortar' as 'explosive shell' comes from the practice of pounding gunpowder inside a cup or globe before lobbing it at the enemy.

[26] Francis Beaumont, *The Knight of the Burning Pestle*, first performed in 1607.

Miraz's wife, Prunaprismia, is another fascinating little example of Lewis's own Martial policy as he composes this tale. We never see Queen Prunaprismia and we are told almost nothing about her, yet she is possessed of this most extraordinary name. Where did it come from and what, if anything, does it have to do with Mars?

As Paul Ford points out,[27] Lewis evidently derived the name from the matronly governess in Charles Dickens's novel, *Little Dorrit*, who instructs her charges to improve their elocution by repeatedly pronouncing the patter, "Papa, potatoes, poultry, prunes, and prism."[28] These words, the governess maintains, "are all very good words for the lips; especially prunes and prism."[29] "Mostly Prunes and Prism" is a chapter title in the second part of the novel.[30] Once we know this connection, we are able to deduce that Lewis's Queen Prunaprismia must be a rather fussy, etiquette-obsessed, school-marmish figure. But there would have been other and simpler ways in which Lewis could have signified such a personality, and nothing comes of her having this sort of personality anyway — so what is the point? Why would Lewis reach into such an obscure corner of Dickens's voluminous output to arrive at this peculiar nomenclature?

The real reason is indeed Martial. Lewis needs a name for the wife of King Miraz. Who is Miraz? The commander of the Telmarine army. What is the top brass in any military chain of command known as? A general. What would the wife of a general be called? Mrs. General. Guess what Dickens's governess is called! "Mrs. General made a

---

[27] Paul F. Ford, *Companion to Narnia* (New York: HarperCollins, 2005), 357.
[28] See Charles Dickens, *Little Dorrit*, book II, ch. 5
[29] Ibid.
[30] Ibid., book II, ch. 7.

sweeping obeisance, and retired with an expression of mouth indicative of Prunes and Prism."[31]

Yet another intriguing name in Prince Caspian is that of Glozelle's horse.[32] We know from the example of Caspian's mount, Destrier, that Lewis chose his equine names in this tale with careful Martial intent; a 'destrier' is defined in the Oxford English Dictionary as a war-horse, a charger. Glozelle's horse is called "Pomely." The name appears only once, when Glozelle refers to "my dappled Pomely,"[33] a tautologous remark, given that the OED defines pomely as "marked with round spots, dappled." But what does the word have to do with Mars?

We have to look one step beyond the word to its literary source. Just as 'Prunaprismia' does not, of itself, imply anything Martial yet understood in its Dickensian context has a nice Martial pay-off, so 'Pomely' does not of itself possess a Martial meaning but takes us thereto if we will follow its lead. Lewis is directing us to his source in Chaucer's *Canterbury Tales*. On this occasion, it is not "The Knight's Tale"[34] that Lewis is plundering but "The Reeve's Tale," where we read:

---

[31] Dickens, *Little Dorrit*, book II, ch. 5.

[32] See Stephen Yandell, "*The Allegory of Love and The Discarded Image*: C.S. Lewis as Medievalist," *C.S. Lewis: Life, Works, and Legacy, Vol. 4: Scholar, Teacher, and Public Intellectual*, ed. Bruce L. Edwards (Santa Barbara, CA: Praeger, 2007), 135.

[33] Lewis, *Prince Caspian*, 399.

[34] In *Planet Narnia* (77), I noted Lewis's admiration for Chaucer's "Knight's Tale," which he calls "a perfect poem of chivalry." Since writing the book I have been made aware of a page of notes, in Lewis's handwriting, in the end-leaves of one of the volumes of his *Complete Chaucer*, in which he says more about "The Knight's Tale" and the planets, and I am grateful to Judith Wolfe for bringing this to my attention and to Bernard O'Donoghue for providing access to the volume in question. The notes reveal Lewis's knowledge of how the planets relate to the days of the week, and I suspect that one of things he is referring to when he says that "the character and influence of the planets are worked into the *Knight's Tale*" is that the tale concludes on a Tuesday, the day of Mars, an appropriate end-point for a tale about Martial knights ("The Knight's Tale," lines 2483-2495). See the HBU website for a picture of the page of Lewis's notes: https://christianthought.hbu.edu/2016/11/19/c-s-lewis-jupiter-and-christmas/.

> This Reve sat upon a ful good stot
> That was al pomely grey and highte Scot.
> A long surcote of pers upon he hade,
> And by his syde he baar a rusty blade.[35]

The Reeve who sits on a pomely horse has a rusty sword. The badly kept weaponry is a sure sign that this Reeve is no true child of Mars, and so, by extension, in the case of Glozelle, we can assume that his armour also must be rusty, simply from the fact that his horse is called 'Pomely'. It's a tell-tale sign of the kind of knight he is. His treacherous comrade-in-arms, Sopespian, reveals how shoddy the Telmarines' armour is when, on seeing Edmund, he exclaims, "What mail he wears! None of our smiths could make the like."[36] Writing elsewhere about the sixteenth-century historian Edward Hall (1499?-1547), Lewis comments:

> A fine armour is almost part of the personality of the knight who wears it; and there was doubtless to [Hall] an almost spiritual significance in the appearance of Richard III's guard at his coronation, "euil appareled and worse harneissed in rusty harneys neither defensable nor skoured to the sale, to the great disdain of all the lookers on."[37]

Lewis, we must remember, had an almost photographic memory. His creative thought-process would, I suspect, have gone something like this: "I need a name for a horse owned by an un-Martial knight. Un-Martial knights have rusty armour. Rusty armour was worn by Chaucer's Reeve. The Reeve's horse was a pomely. So

---

[35] In modern English, we might gloss these lines as follows: "This Reeve sat upon a very fine horse / That was all dappled grey and called 'Scot'. / He had on a long outer coat of dark blue, / And by his side he bore a rusty sword" ("General Prologue," lines 615ff).

[36] Lewis, *Prince Caspian*, 399.

[37] C.S. Lewis, *English Literature in the Sixteenth Century Excluding Drama* (Oxford: Clarendon Press, 1954), 279.

let us name the horse Pomely." Lewis believed that success in writing came about by suggestion, not statement. He was not always aware how unusually retentive his memory was and may have overestimated his readers' ability to make the sort of instantaneous connections that he was able to form. But much of the time, I believe, he is deliberately setting a puzzle for his readers first of all to sense and then, if they wish, to try and solve.

As we end this examination of *Prince Caspian*, I must mention an episode which is at first sight indebted not to Mars but to the Moon. It occurs after the climactic battle when the victorious Narnian forces are treated by Aslan to a celebratory banquet:

> Thus Aslan feasted the Narnians till long after the sunset had died away, and the stars had come out ... The best thing of all about this feast was that there was no breaking up or going away, but as the talk grew quieter and slower, one after another would begin to nod and finally drop off to sleep with feet toward the fire and good friends on either side, till at last there was silence all round the circle ... But all night Aslan and the Moon gazed upon each other with joyful and unblinking eyes.[38]

A critic of my thesis has pointed out that this scene seems much more obviously Lunar than Martial. Why does Aslan not stare at the Narnian equivalent of Mars, which is apparently named "Tarva, the Lord of Victory"?[39] On the surface, that is a fair criticism, but it is open to two rejoinders, one general, one particular.

In general, we must note — to state the obvious — that all the events of the tale happen either during the day

---

[38] Lewis, *Prince Caspian*, 414.
[39] Ibid., 338.

or during the night. This does not mean that all events must be either Solar or Lunar; the other five planets, of course, work in consort with the two great lights. According to the Book of Genesis, the Sun 'rules' the day and the Moon 'rules' the night, but, as the long tradition of Christian astrology testifies, this rulership does not entail the exclusion of other planetary influences. Furthermore, "in a certain juncture of the planets each may play the other's part."[40]

In particular, Mars was understood by Lewis to be the sponsor of vigilance. In *Perelandra*, when Ransom beholds the Oyarsa of Mars, we read: "Malacandra seemed to him to have the look of one standing armed, at the ramparts of his own remote archaic world, in ceaseless vigilance, his eyes ever roaming the earthward horizon whence his danger came long ago."[41] In *That Hideous Strength*, at the descent of the Martial god, we read that "Ransom knew, as a man knows when he touches iron, the clear, taut splendour of that celestial spirit who now flashed between them: vigilant Malacandra, captain of a cold orb, whom men call Mars."[42]

It is in this context that we should read the passage about Aslan and the Moon gazing all night upon each other with unblinking eyes. A vigil is being kept; it is a Martial moment, albeit communicated by means of Lunar imagery. All the other characters fall asleep, but Aslan, like an alert sentry or watchful soldier on a castle rampart, does his Martial duty, guarding his people. Lewis is giving us a planetary spin on Psalm 121, where the Lord of Hosts

---

[40] C.S. Lewis, Letter to A.K. Hamilton Jenkin, November 4, 1925.
[41] C.S. Lewis, *Perelandra* (New York: Scribner, 2003), 172.
[42] C. S. Lewis, *That Hideous Strength* (New York: Scribner, 2003), 322.

ceaselessly oversees his faithful ones: "He that keepeth thee will not slumber. Behold, he that keepeth Israel shall neither slumber nor sleep . . . The sun shall not smite thee by day, nor the moon by night."[43]

The Martial meanings I have tried to unearth in this article are all highly involved. There is subtlety and indirectness at play, so much so that some readers may be inclined to dismiss it as too complex to be believed. But this would be to overlook how in much medieval art there is "the love of the labyrinthine; the tendency to offer to the mind or the eye something that cannot be taken in at a glance, something that at first looks planless though all is planned. Everything leads to everything else, but by very intricate paths."[44]

As a medievalist himself, Lewis naturally enough reflected this imaginative grasp of reality in his own fictional writings. The Martial details we have examined here, though admittedly minor and unobvious, are not negligible. They are rather, as Lewis puts it in a poem, "patterned atoms," basic and essential components of those "woven mazes" out of which the cosmos is built.[45] Since God has created a universe in which every particle of matter matters, a Christian writer, fulfilling his sub-creative role, must likewise make every word count. Speaking of Dante's microscopically fine artistry in *The Divine Comedy*, Lewis declared: "It is just on such apparent *minutiae* that the total effect of a poem depends."[46] The names of Caspian, and Miraz, and Prunaprismia, and Pomely, and

---

[43] Ps. 121:3-4, 7.
[44] Lewis, *The Discarded Image*, 194.
[45] C.S. Lewis, "Le Roi S'Amuse," *Poems*, ed. Walter Hooper (New York: HarperCollins, 1994), 37-38. For my commentary on this poem, see: http://www.cslewis.com/a-look-at-lewiss-poetry-2/.
[46] C.S. Lewis, "A Note on Comus," *Studies in Medieval and Renaissance Literature*, 181.

Aslan's unblinking gaze at the Moon — these things contribute to the Martial atmosphere of the second Narnia Chronicle. Without some careful archaeological digging we won't notice exactly how they conspire to this end, but once we press into the work we see that, like a stick of rock, wherever you cut it open, it spells MARS.

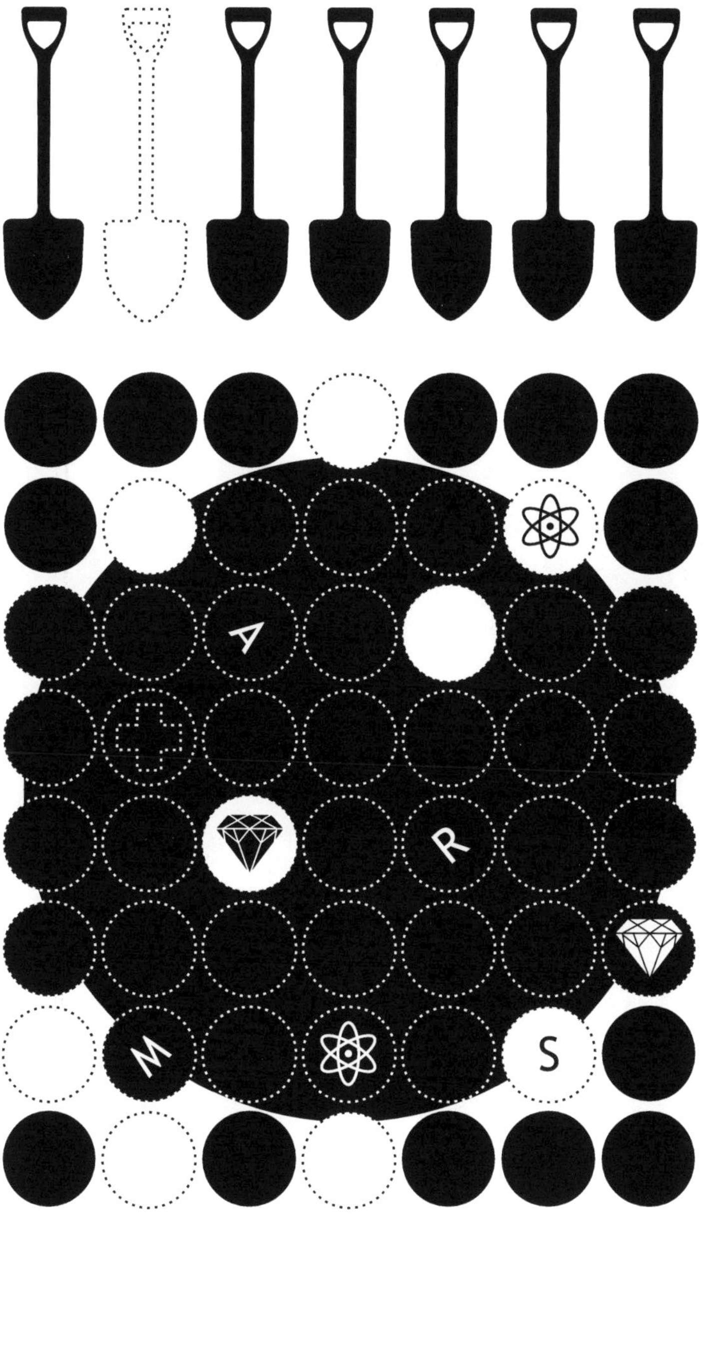
A
R
M
S

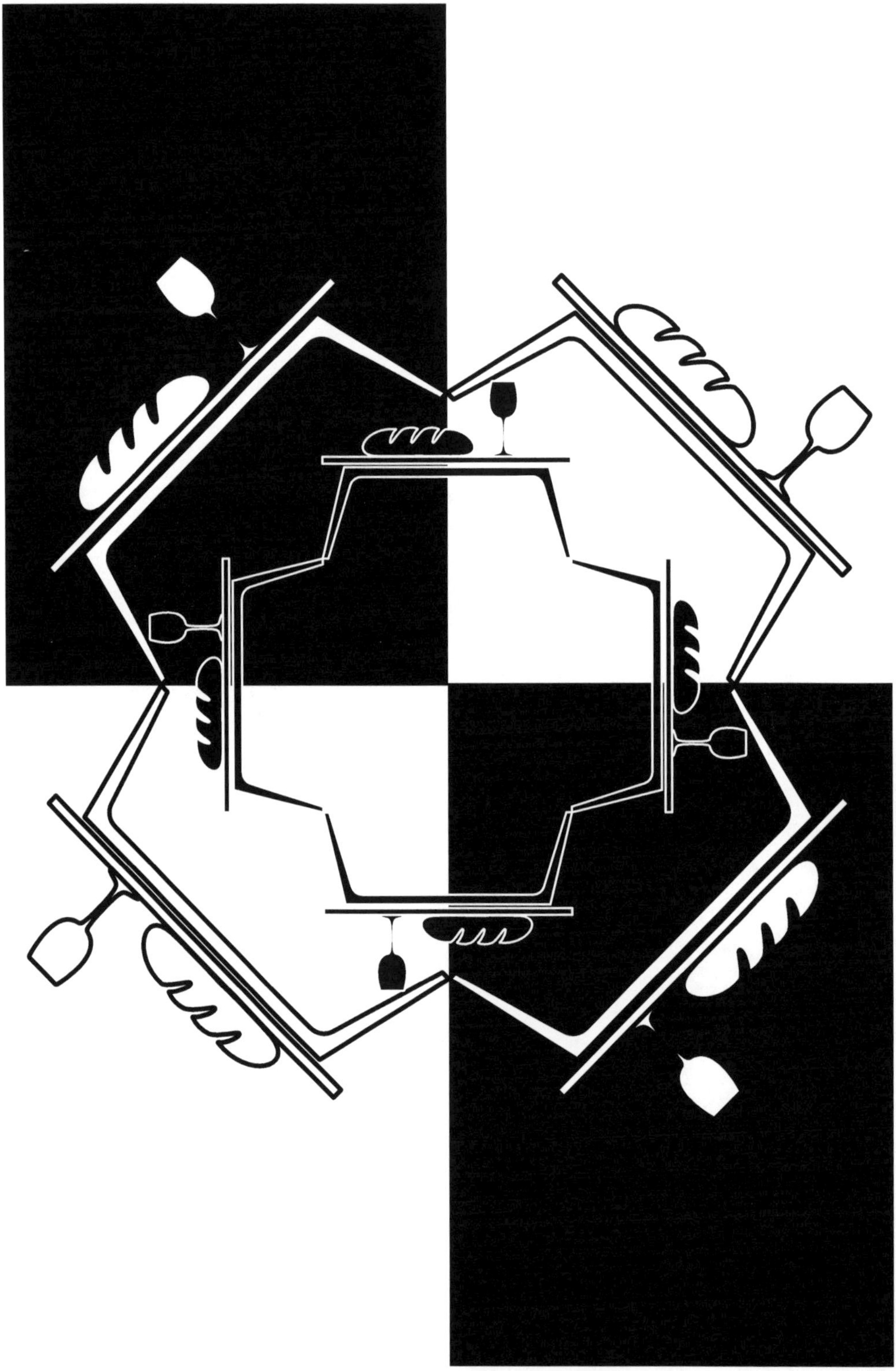

Table Narnia:
Fugue to Evangelical Adventure

Kyoko Yuasa

The Stone Table where Aslan dies in C.S. Lewis's *The Lion, the Witch and the Wardrobe* is generally interpreted as a symbol of Christ's Cross. However, the Table, as it appears in the first three books of the Narnian series, reveals a more complex meaning through a fugue-like repetition of two images: first, Aslan on the Table and second, the "table" itself with its possible history prior to Aslan's death and its fate after His resurrection. The counterpoint of these two images reveals the mysticism of evangelical adventure to the Narnian travelers.

This fugue-like repetition is reflected in the various stories about the Table, its unsolved mythology and the visible completion of the Gospel. Lewis uses the adjectives "visible" and "unsolved" to denote two types of miracle: Christ's death and resurrection is a "visible" type, while the pagan mythology of Corn King or death and resurrection of the corn is not visible, so "still unsolved."[1] Regarding the echoing pattern of both the "visible" message of Christianity and the "unsolved" prophecy of mythology, Lewis uses the musical term "fugue" to compare the intertwined harmony of miracles to the reality of God: "Divine reality is like a fugue. All His acts are different, but they all rhyme or echo to one another, the liveness, the elusiveness, the intertwined harmonies."[2] This intertwined

---

[1] C.S. Lewis, "Miracles," in *God in the Dock* (Grand Rapids, MI: Wm. B. Eerdmans, 2014), 22, 13.
[2] Ibid., 23.

fugal harmony may be found in Lewis's assertion that there is one Great Story, the "visible," which transcends human stories of myth, the "unsolved." He believes that the myths of pagan gods, dead and risen, were historically completed in the Gospel, the story of Jesus Christ who died and rose 2000 years ago.[3]

To express his Christian ideas through his fictional works, Lewis uses a fugue-type method such as is commonly found in postmodernist literature. I have elsewhere termed Lewis's characteristic literary approach "Christian Postmodernism."[4] Lewis adopts various literary approaches including the employment of multiple metafiction-style stories, the creation of a frame story, the blurring of the roles of narrator, author, and character, and the intrusion of the narrator as persona "I." His use of a frame story or metafiction reflects his notion of the Gospel in which myth is beyond reason and thought.[5] He starts *The Lion, the Witch and The Wardrobe* (LWW) with the form of a frame story in which the Pevensies are transported from this world into another world. Similarly, the Table is first introduced through a frame story when Caspian's adventure is recounted to the Pevensies by Trumpkin.

The narrator of *The Chronicles* is also a character or persona in the stories.[6] Its gender is not certain, but I provisionally use the male pronoun, for the voice sounds like a mixture of Lewis, Prof. Kirk, and an unknown third

---

[3] C.S. Lewis, *The Collected Letters of C.S. Lewis Volume I: Family Letters 1905-1931* (New York: Harper, 2004), 970.

[4] Kyoko Yuasa, *C.S. Lewis and Christian Postmodernism: Word, Image, and Beyond* (Eugene: Wipf and Stock, 2016), 46-47.

[5] Ibid., 111.

[6] Ibid.

person. He usually keeps his objective stance as narrator but on rare occasions interludes the story, directly speaking to the reader. His voice is sometimes marked with parentheses: "None of the party except Edmund (and perhaps Trumpkin) was a rock climber."[7] He also directly speaks with a character of the story: "'Why,' said I, 'was it so sad?' 'Sad!! No,' said Lucy."[8] The persona "I" acts both as a narrator and a character, and his ambiguous roles blur between fact and fiction.

Lewis's ultimate intention in using these various fugue-like techniques is to express a greater story that is beyond understanding. Lewis compares the divine reality to fugue. Just as God completed a beautiful miracle of the Gospel by mobilizing all his visible and invisible myths, so a fugue likewise creates a beautiful harmony made up of different parts that echo to one another. Lewis makes the fugue effect in Narnia by paralleling two stories of the Table, known and unknown, and also including a story of the Table in a frame story.

The beautiful quality of fugue in Narnia can be rephrased as its "Donegality" — Lewis's concept as re-evaluated by Michael Ward in his book *Planet Narnia*. Ward's work focuses on the atmospheric flavor of The Chronicles of Narnia: "Surveying the various words which Lewis uses to denote *ipseitas*, I propose to elect 'Donegality' for this particular destiny."[9] Lewis coined the term "Donegality" in his work *Spenser's Image of Life* to encapsulate the significance of the spiritual essence that draws readers to repeatedly return to and re-read the

---
[7] C.S. Lewis, *Prince Caspian* (New York: Harper, 1980), 129.
[8] C.S. Lewis, *The Voyage of the Dawn Treader* (New York: Harper, 1980), 265.
[9] Michael Ward, *Planet Narnia: The Seven Heavens in the Imagination of C.S. Lewis* (New York: Oxford University Press, 2010), 74.

same stories. As Ward explains, "Re-reading them is like going back to a fruit for its taste; to an air for ... what? for *itself*; to a region for its whole atmosphere — to Donegal for its Donegality and London for its Londonness."[10] Ward offers no direct observations regarding the Table, and indeed few scholars speak of its significance. Paul Ford, however, envisions the heavenly communion when he sees the renewed feast and the Knife on Aslan's table in *The Voyage of the Dawn Treader*. He associates the table with the Holy Grail in the Arthurian legends: "the eternal refreshment of the Eucharist as the heavenly banquet."[11] Colin Duriez sees several Celtic cultural elements in Narnia and connects the Stone Table with Celtic *cromlechs*. He focuses on "a transfiguration of the pagan by the Christian."[12] Neither Ford nor Duriez, however, appears to note the different representations of 'table' and 'Table' in *The Voyage Dawn Treader* (VDT). For example, Ford capitalizes "Table,"[13] although it is expressed as "Aslan's table" in VDT.[14]

The Table in The Lion, the Witch and the Wardrobe

In LWW, the Table, reminiscent of death, ultimately offers the joy of resurrection. It visibly represents a jovial festivity for Lucy who was "laughing, though she didn't know why."[15] Aslan delightedly and playfully races with Lucy and Susan beside the Table. "Round and round the hill-top he led them."[16] Aslan continues to play another

---

[10] Ward, *Planet Narnia*, 115.
[11] Paul F. Ford, *Companion to Narnia* (San Francisco: HarperSanFrancisco, 1994), 64.
[12] Colin Duriez, *A Field Guide to Narnia* (Downers Grove, IL: InterVarsity Press, 2004), 211.
[13] Ford, *Companion to Narnia*, 64.
[14] Lewis, *Dawn Treader*, 215.
[15] C. S. Lewis, *The Lion, the Witch, and the Wardrobe* (New York: Harper, 1980), 225.
[16] Ibid.

game of tossing Lucy and Susan, like a ball, in the air: "whether it was more like playing with a thunderstorm or playing with a kitten Lucy could never make up her mind."[17]

However, the Table is initially introduced first by the Beavers and then the White Witch indirectly in LWW. Although in the beginning, the four children are unaware of either Aslan or the Table, three of them (with the exception of Edmund) choose to trust the Beavers who tell them to go to the Table. One significant reason for this is Lucy's handkerchief, which Mr. Tumnus had entrusted to Mr. Beaver, telling him to meet Lucy "if anything happened to him."[18] It may also stem from the spiritual feelings they experience on hearing Aslan's name, "for once again that strange feeling—like the first signs of spring, like good news, had come over them."[19] Something awe-inspiring tells them that the Table is their only way to save Mr. Tumnus, and later Edmund, from the White Witch.

The Table is visibly presented to the reader, as well as to the Pevensies, in the latter part of the book. It is described by the narrator as a table-shaped stone construction that "was cut all over with strange lines and figures that might be the letters of an unknown language."[20] It is uncertain, however, who built the Table or why it was built. At this point in the narrative, although the lines and figures on the Table remain undeciphered, they exert a mysterious force on the travelers, as the

---

[17] C.S. Lewis, *The Lion, the Witch, and the Wardrobe*, 225.
[18] Ibid., 73.
[19] Ibid., 111.
[20] Ibid., 173.

narrator says, "They gave you a curious feeling when you looked at them."[21]

The age of the Stone Table is also unknown, but the White Witch has some knowledge of what is written on the Table. She appears to associate herself with the Norse god Odin. According to H.A. Guerber, who wrote histories of Norse mythology and was particularly influential on Lewis, Odin learns the secret of the magic runes by sacrificing himself, using his spear made of ash wood.[22] The Witch invokes Odin when she refers to both "a spear" and "ash": "Tell you what is written in letters deep as a spear is long on the trunk of the World Ash Tree?"[23] She seems to know something of the letters on the Table, at least the meaning of the Deep Magic. She asserts, "I have a right to kill a traitor."[24] Unlike Odin, however, who has come to gain the secret runes at the risk of his life, the Witch does not know the deeper meaning of the invisible letters, the Deeper Magic. As Aslan later explains, "If a willing victim who had committed no treachery was killed in a traitor's stead, the Table would crack and Death itself would start working backwards."[25]

The White Witch assumes that the Table's purpose is for killing victims, for "that is where it [sacrifice] has always been done before."[26] Lewis does not clarify whether these other victims were killed by the White Witch or someone else. Devin Brown assumes that the victims were killed by the Witch on the Table, but "whether these other victims

---

[21] Lewis, *The Lion, the Witch, and the Wardrobe*, 173.
[22] H. A. Guerber, *Myths of the Norsemen: From the Eddas and Sagas*. (London: George C. Harrap, 1908), 16, 33.
[23] Lewis, *The Lion, the Witch, and the Wardrobe*, 195.
[24] Ibid., 155.
[25] Ibid., 179.
[26] Ibid., 148.

were traitors she had a right to kill or simply creatures she wanted dead is another aspect Lewis leaves unexplained."[27] The Table is described in negative terms as "a great grim slab." Lewis includes this harsh element in his portrayal of the Table to emphasize it as an appropriate place for sacrifice. As Brown indicates, the word "grim … adds a somewhat paradoxical emotional coloring."[28]

Lewis must owe something in his portrayal of the Table's harshness to the image of the megalithic site, Stonehenge. Although Vaus points out that there is no evidence that human or animal sacrifice occurred at Stonehenge, we may conjecture that Stonehenge would have provided Lewis with imaginative inspiration.[29] Before Lewis converted to Christianity around 1931, he had had two kinds of strange experiences relating to the Stonehenge. One relates to a short story that he wrote about Stonehenge in 1916, an eerie tale called "The Meagre One," and the second was an actual visit that he made to Stonehenge in 1925. While he does not speak directly of either Deep Magic or Deeper Magic, these experiences must have elicited some spiritual response in Lewis, a sense of what Rudolph Otto called, "the numinous," a feeling of awe mixed with fear.[30] In "The Meagre One" the main character is punished at Stonehenge for killing a spider, and he seems to derive a masochistic pleasure from tormenting himself. "No, the Meagre One was not born with a squint: but long, long,

---

[27] Devin Brown, *Inside Narnia: A Guide to Exploring The Lion, the Witch and the Wardrobe* (Grand Rapids: Baker, 2005), 187.

[28] Ibid., 168.

[29] Will Vaus, "Lewis and Stonehenge," *The Official Website of C.S. Lewis*, 17 October, 2018, accessed 30 November, 2018, http://www.cslewis.com/lewis-and-stonehenge/.

[30] Rudolph Otto, *The Idea of the Holy* (New York: Penguin, 1959), 151.

long ago, so long ago that Stonehenge had a roof and walls & was a new built temple, he killed a spider."[31]

Lewis visited Stonehenge on Salisbury Plain in 1925, he wrote afterwards that he was shocked to hear the disgusting roar of military exercise around the field. "It was the first time I had heard a gun fired since I left France, and I cannot tell you how odd the sensation was."[32] Salisbury Plain is a unique site that hosts both prehistoric monuments and modern military exercises. A large portion of the plain has been used for military exercises since 1898. The sound of the army reminded Lewis of his grim days as an officer of the Third Battalion in France from 1917 to 1918.

In the story of "The Meagre One" set at Stonehenge, Lewis seemed to express himself as a slave to self-hatred, and on hearing the blasts in the vicinity of the Stonehenge, he must have felt experienced displeasure at the dehumanization caused by the modern technological age, though he simply expressed it as "odd." Around three decades later, perhaps Lewis may have converted these negative emotions into a positive redeeming energy in LWW, just as he transformed the meanings of the Table from the site for Aslan's death to His resurrection. He recreated the splitting sound of the Table in a new dimension. As the Table cracked it sounded the blast of Aslan's redeeming sacrifice for Edmund, who was then a slave to self-hatred: "a loud noise — a great cracking, deafening noise as if a giant had broken a giant's plate."[33] Aslan's redeeming energy extends from the Table to the

---

[31] Lewis, *The Collected Letters*, 259.
[32] Ibid., 640.
[33] Lewis, *The Lion, the Witch, and the Wardrobe*, 186.

rest of the natural world, which was locked in slavery to the White Witch. The redeeming sound of the Table echoes the roar of Aslan when renewing the wood in Narnia: "... all the trees in front of him bend before the blast of his roaring as grass bends in a meadow before the wind."[34]

The Table in Prince Caspian

Prince Caspian (PC) opens with the four children's pilgrimage to the Table. Like medieval pilgrims journeying to venerate the relics of a saint, the four travelers pay a visit to Aslan's relics. However, the Pevensies visit not the tomb of a dead saint, but a tomb-like mound in which the Table is buried. They do not see Aslan's body or bones there, but they meet the living Aslan on the way to the burial mound. When they see "the Great Mound"[35] from a distance, Aslan himself appears to the travelers, reminiscent of Jesus joining his disciples as they walked to Emmaus.[36] The Narnian travelers realize that reaching the Table is not their ultimate purpose, but actually meeting Aslan is the true goal. A pilgrimage or journey towards the relics of the Table serves as a spiritual aid that motivates them to meet Aslan.

On meeting Aslan, Prince Caspian and the travelers are given individual missions. Lucy and Susan help the King of the Wood to rescue his woods, and soon they see the trees again walking and dancing. The boys and the dwarf help Prince Caspian and the old Narnians fight against the usurping Narnian dictator, Miraz. Aslan tells Peter, Edmund, and Trumpkin to go to the Mound and to

---

[34] Lewis, *The Lion, the Witch, and the Wardrobe*, 180.
[35] Lewis, *Prince Caspian*, 161.
[36] C. S. Lewis, *The C. S. Lewis Bible* (New York: HarperCollins, 2010), 1184.

"deal with what you will find there."[37] Like the Celtic pilgrims who visited "burial grounds as gateways to the other life,"[38] the Pevensies' journey ultimately seems to offer access to Aslan, the eternal being, unlimited by time and untamed by space.

During the first ten chapters of PC, the role of the Table is not fully explained for the reader. The burial mound is referred to as "Aslan's How" in PC, but no reason is given as to why it was built, though the narrator offers some small glimpses into its long history. The How is connected to LWW explicitly when "the children could see the Great Mound, Aslan's How, which had been raised over the Table since their days."[39] The word *how* is Old English for 'mound', and its usage, Duriez notes, reminds us of "the sweep of Narnia's history."[40]

The How is only mentioned to the reader by a mythological creature, the dwarf Trumpkin. Lewis presents the tale of Trumpkin in the form of a frame story, within which the stories of Cornelius and Caspian are included. Listening to Trumpkin, the four children — and the reader — come to regard Aslan's How as Aslan's Table, but they do not fully understand the difference. Edmund sounds somewhat confused: "We'll be at the Stone Table (Aslan's How, I mean)."[41] They are as yet unaware of the danger for they do not clearly understand the 1300 years of change that Narnia has experienced. Their lack of understanding engenders confusion. Geographically they are lost in the

---

[37] Lewis, *Prince Caspian*, 164.
[38] Philip Sheldrake, *Living Between Worlds: Place and Journey in Celtic Spirituality* (Cambridge, MA: Cowley Publications, 1995), 55.
[39] Lewis, *Prince Caspian*, 164.
[40] Duriez, *A Field Guide to Narnia*, 170.
[41] Lewis, *Prince Caspian*, 125.

gorge, while spiritually they cannot trust Lucy, who has seen Aslan. Peter, their leader, makes the wrong decision to disregard his sister and admits, "I know Lucy may be right after all, but I can't help it."[42]

Trumpkin, the children's main supporter on their journey, adds another confusing element. As the dwarf is skeptical of the existence of Aslan, he appears oblivious to the Table's significance. Although the reader has good reason to disbelieve Trumpkin, he is nonetheless a loyal servant to his master Prince Caspian who does trust Aslan. Both the Pevensies and the reader must decide whether or not they can trust their guide.

Within Trumpkin's story, we hear another tale of Aslan's How from the mythological creature, Cornelius, who explains to the other Narnians that Aslan's How was built by Narnians long ago: "Narnians raised in very ancient times over a very magical place, where stood—and perhaps still stands—a very magical Stone."[43] Although Cornelius, half-human and half-dwarf and presumably not believed by Trumpkin, emphasizes the magical nature of the Stone Table when he shares the story of the burial with the Narnians for the first time, he has never seen the site nor Aslan himself.

Through Trumpkin's story, we hear about the impression that the mound makes on Caspian. Although the Prince does not know the exact date of its construction, the narrator describes the sense of awe surrounding the ancient mound: "a round green hill on top of another hill, long since grown over with trees, and one little, low doorway leading into it. The tunnels inside

---

[42] Lewis, *Prince Caspian*, 134.
[43] Ibid., 136.

were a perfect maze till you got to know them, and they were lined and roofed with smooth stones."[44] Through the narrator's voice, we, the reader, also see what Caspian saw: "Caspian saw strange characters and snaky patterns, and pictures in which the form of a Lion was repeated again and again."[45]

This description of the mound, inside and outside, evokes Newgrange, a prehistoric megalithic mound in the country of Lewis's birth. It is a hill-like burial in Ireland, around fifty kilometers from Dublin, with an entrance stone engraved with curved lines and a straight tunnel of stones concealed inside the mound. The site is best known for the illumination of its tunnel by the winter solstice sun. In PC, Aslan appears to the travelers, not like the sunshine, but like moonlight at midnight, yet he illuminates their minds as would the solstice sunshine at Newgrange, showing them which way to go. "Aslan without hesitation led them to their left, farther up the gorge…. Fortunately the Moon shone right above the gorge so that neither side was in shadow."[46]

The Table was deliberately made inaccessible, buried in the hill, and covered by the wood. It is likely that this measure was taken to prevent some people from using the inspirational place to satisfy their own ambitions, perhaps because the Table was sacred. The dwarf Nikabrik provides a good sample of using the Table for self-serving purposes. His true character is ambiguously veiled while still outside Aslan's How but is gradually revealed inside the mound. When he looks at the Table in the mound, he

---

[44] Lewis, *Prince Caspian*, 137.
[45] Ibid.
[46] Ibid., 160.

thinks not of Aslan, sacrificed on the Table, but rather remembers the White Witch who killed Aslan. He is possessed of an evil desire to use the Table as a tool to gain power. He says, "We want power: and we want a power that will be on our side. As for power, do not the stories say that the Witch defeated Aslan, and bound him, and killed him on that very stone which is over there, just beyond the light?"[47]

Through stories related by mythological creatures, both Trumpkin, the cynical but loyal subject of Caspian, and Cornelius, the staunch believer in Aslan, the grand narrative of the Table is told and retold in the manner of a fugue, and finally its truth is mysteriously passed to the children and the reader, just as the smaller mythologies of ancient man reach completion the Grand Story of the Gospel.

The Table in The Voyage of the Dawn Treader

In VDT, the word 'table' is defined as "a wide oblong space" and is represented in two ways.[48] Lewis writes about the table with a lower-case 't' while at other times, it appears as Table, with a capital 'T'. In Chapters 13 and 14 of VDT, the table with a small 't', is mentioned 22 times, excluding the pronoun 'it'. The fugue-like counterpoint of two images ultimately allows the voyagers to experience the evangelical adventure.

There are two noteworthy contexts in which it is referred to as an ordinary 'table'. The first is when the crew sees three sleepers who had been enchanted as retribution for their blasphemous self-assertion leading to

---

[47] Lewis, *Prince Caspian*, 177.
[48] Lewis, *The Voyage of The Dawn Treader*, 207.

their insulting the Stone Knife.[49] The other is when a retired sky-star, Ramandu, and his daughter specify the flat stone space as "Aslan's table."[50]

The Table — with a capital "T" — is represented when Lucy remembers it as the place where Aslan was killed, though she does not directly point to the oblong space. She seems to be uncomfortable when she hears the lady speak about the rectangular space as Aslan's table: "'Why is it called Aslan's table?' asked Lucy presently."[51] Although the lady explains that the table is called Aslan's table because it has been set at Aslan's order, the travelers continue to call it the 'table'. They are reluctant to change their views even at the end of chapter 14. This is likely to result from the travelers' lack of understanding as to what the stone table is for. They may perhaps suppose that this 'table' is not the 'Table' because it seems illogical to think of Aslan's Table being set on the island of stars. It also seems physically impossible to think that the intact table could be Aslan's Table, which has been split in two. It seems as though the travelers are under the control of an enchantment that must be broken. They need to see beyond to the invisible reality to unfold the remainder of the complete story. The narrator of VDT has a different perspective to that of the travelers on the flat space, referring to it twice at the end of chapter 14: "they all came trooping back to Aslan's Table"[52] and "they all ate and drank together at the great Table between the pillars where the feast was magically renewed."[53] Ramandu

---

[49] Lewis, *The Voyage of The Dawn Treader*, 215.
[50] Ibid., 229.
[51] Ibid., 217.
[52] Ibid., 311.
[53] Ibid., 313.

predicts that the enchantment that has been placed on the sleepers will be broken when the travelers journey east and return to the island of stars. Ramandu's prediction may also prove true for the travelers' lack of understanding, though it is not explicitly suggested that they will gain this perspective by which the table becomes the Table.

In the first two books of *The Chronicles of Narnia*, the Table is the destination that the travelers seek, but in the third book, VDT, the travelling companions are unaware how intrinsic the Table is to their voyage. Unlike in LWW and PC, there is no foreshadowing of the Table before chapters 13 and 14 of VDT. However, Lewis describes both chapters as though they were the foreshadowing of the three dramas in Chapter 16: the crew return to save the sleepers, a mouse-knight Reepicheep is left alone to save them and to journey possibly to Aslan's Country, and three visitors from Earth reach the island of the Lamb.

Even after the travelers have discovered the whereabouts of the seven missing lords, they continue to sail to the end of the eastern sea. The primary reason for doing this is to break the enchantment that has been placed on the sleepers, as a mythological Ramandu guided their fate. It is also likely that the underlying reason is to break their own enchantment. On returning to the island of stars, the voyagers will probably see the merging of two images: sleepers and themselves, awakened. Then they can gain the restored sight of the Table.

The other voyagers can gain renewed perspective of the Table in different ways. Reepicheep is a reflection of Aslan at the Table who sacrificed himself to save Narnia. The noble mouse receives Ramandu's prediction as a personal oracle: someone must be left behind to save the enchanted sleepers. The small knight whose life is guided by a dryad's prophecy, is finally lifted up upon the waves, possibly to Aslan's Country.

Aslan himself does not visibly appear at the Table on the island of stars, but He comes in the form of the Lamb at the next island and prepares breakfast for the children. While the travelers eat breakfast with the Lamb, they can see the Lamb's transformation into Aslan, reminiscent of two disciples who recognized their companion as Jesus when they sat at meal with Him.[54] They will be visibly at Aslan's Table, though "the Table" is not explicitly mentioned in the text. They are opened to the intrinsic image of "the Table" while they eat.

The sharing of a meal with Jesus also reminds us of "the Lord's Table" the day before Jesus was offered as the Lamb for Sacrifice. The Eucharist is a temporal feast to "proclaim the Lord's death until he comes."[55] However, in the coming Kingdom of God we will have an eternal feast with the Lord.[56] The children's sharing of "the Table" is an invisible but prophetic vision of the eternal feast with the Lamb.

As evangelism is the saving of sleeping souls abroad and at home, so the crew on the ship in VDT returns to break the enchantment that has been placed on the sleepers, Reepicheep gives himself up to save others, and the visitors from Earth willingly share the invisible Table with the Lamb. The children finally come to understand that the real reason why they have come to Narnia is so that they may know Aslan in their own home country, and

---

[54] Lk 24:30-31, NRSV.
[55] 1 Cor. 11:26, NRSV.
[56] Rev. 3:20, NRSV.

evangelize themselves in Narnia and to others on the earth.

The counterpoint of two images of the Table creates a fugue, that rhyme or echo to one another, intertwined harmonies, revealing to us that being with Aslan is the real reason for our adventure in Narnia, just as being with Jesus is the real reason for our adventure in this world. Like the two disciples at Emmaus who recognized Jesus at the table, the eyes of the Narnian travelers are opened to the mysticism of evangelical adventure through the Table. As Underhill finds the transcendent life revealed "in all those places where the direct and simple life of earth goes on," the evangelical truth may be found at the most common facet of life, the Table.[57]

---

[57] Evelyn Underhill, "Mysticism," *Christian Classics Ethereal Library*, accessed 17 October, 2018, http://www.ccel.org/ccel/underhill/mysticism.pdf?membership_type=b10f8d8331236b8b61aa39bc6f86075c12d7e005.

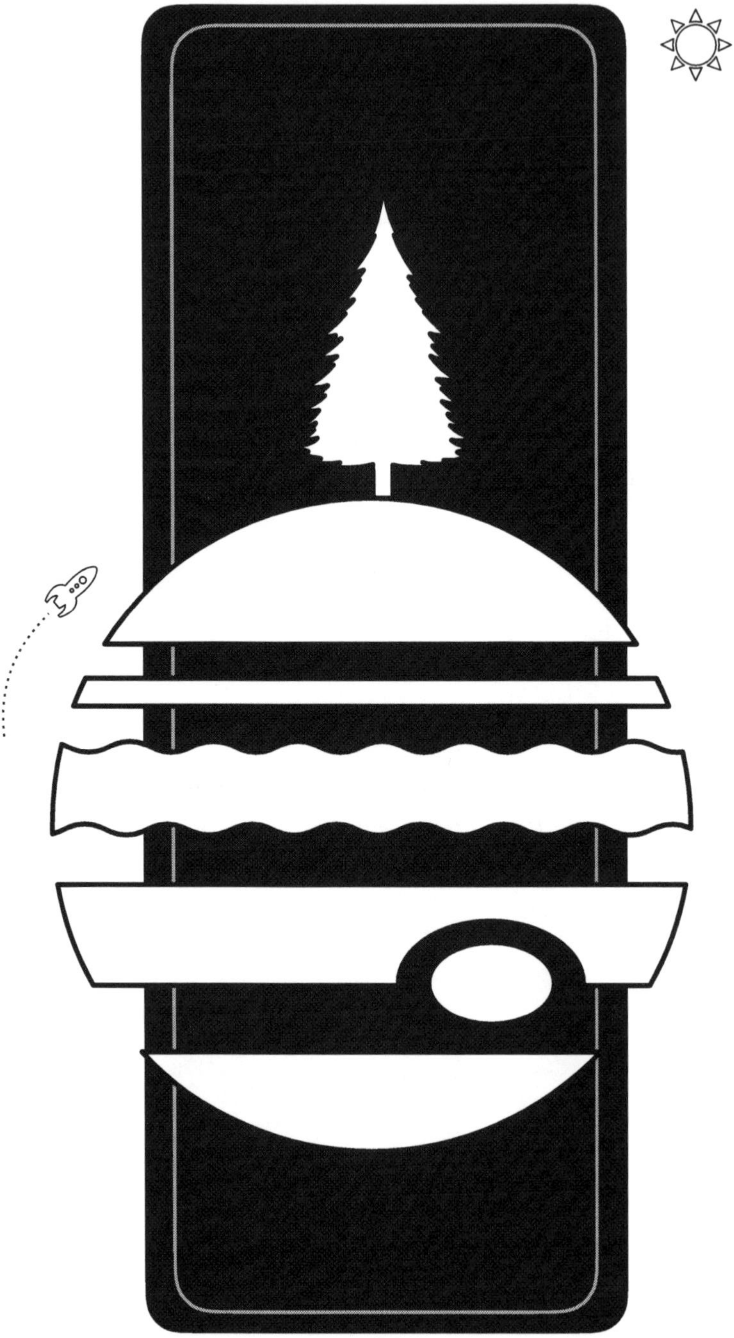

The Cure Has Begun:

Salvation as Illuminated by the Planetary Imagery in The Chronicles of Narnia

Annie Crawford

Like most fairy tales, *The Chronicles of Narnia* are salvation stories. As the parables of Jesus demonstrate, salvation is communicated best through a story because the Gospel is itself the great tale of rescue and restoration. Just as a marriage is much more than just an exchange of vows, so too our salvation in Christ is much more than a spiritual transaction; it is the multifaceted, storied truth of our cosmic redemption! It is the restoration of all things to divine order and right relationship with God. Through the form of fairy tale, C.S. Lewis crafted his Narnian *Chronicles* to give his readers an imaginative experience of this cosmic redemption. In his seminal work, *Planet Narnia*, Michael Ward revealed the framework of medieval cosmology that Lewis used to subtly shape the symbolism in each of his seven salvation stories. Lewis explored the multidimensional, cosmic nature of salvation by composing seven different fairy tales shaped by the imagery of the seven different medieval planets. Ward's decoding of this planetary imagery enables Lewis's readers to better understand Narnia's richly varying visions of Christ's one great salvation.

In the first Chronicle, *The Lion, the Witch, and The Wardrobe*, Lewis employs the imagery of King Jupiter to portray the cosmic stage upon which salvation's great story is played. The entire cosmos is created to be rightly ordered in wondrous submission to its Creator who alone is the source of all goodness, truth, beauty, and being. However, evil entered the cosmos on the day the Son of Dawn fell from heaven and tore open the fabric of reality in his desire for an independent throne "above the stars of God."[1] In *The Lion*, Lewis uses the high, distant, and cold symbolism of Saturn in contrast with the jocund, magnanimous, and joyful symbolism of Jupiter to embody this cosmic war between the Satanic reign of the White Witch and the redemptive rule of the Holy Lion. By comparing the Narnian stories to "The Planets," an early poem where Lewis develops his understanding of each planet's power and character, Ward deepens our understanding of how Lewis envisioned the battle between Aslan and the White Witch. Like Saturn, who devoured his own children to prevent the rise of a new kingdom, the Witch brings "pale pestilence" and makes Narnia "Sickly and uncertain" and "Weak with winters."[2] But the reign of bright Jupiter, the true King, ascends with the return of the golden Aslan. The Jovial King brings "winter passed" and "righteous power" as he restores order in the land with "joy and jubilee."[3]

It is within this great cosmic narrative that we can clearly see Edmund's individual story of redemption. Long before the Pevensies entered the Wardrobe, the cosmic war between the Saturnocentric tyrant and the Jovial King cut through their hearts. Before Edmund's foot felt one

---

[1] Isa. 14:12-13.
[2] C.S. Lewis, "The Planets," in *Poems*, ed. Walter Hooper (San Diego: Harcourt, Inc., 1992), 14-15.
[3] Ibid., 14.

crunch of Narnian snow, he demonstrated a grumbling, deceptive, and Saturnine spirit. On their first night in the great house in England, Edmund "was tired and pretending not to be tired, which always made him bad-tempered."[4] His attitude was sour and his sibling relationships tainted. While Peter warm-heartedly tries to encourage and care for Lucy, Edmund "could be spiteful," and he taunted his sister cruelly before he ever came under the White Witch's particular power.[5] Edmund resists being influenced by Peter's cheerful, magnanimous spirit because he bitterly resented his place as the younger brother.

Edmund's Saturnocentric orientation made him vulnerable to the White Witch's power. She promised to make him the king of a different dynasty so he need not forever submit to his older brother. The usurping White Queen promises to make Edmund the "King of Narnia when I am gone" but only make his brother "a Duke and your sisters Duchesses."[6] Edmund enjoys the deceptive delights of the Queen's power and falls under her spell. The great lie enters his disordered heart and, like the treacherous Son of the Dawn, he lives set his own "throne on high."[7] He turns traitor against the true King and betrays his brother and sisters to the White Witch.

To be saved, Edmund must be released from the treacherous power of the White Witch and reoriented to the Jovian spirit of Aslan who is the true and eternal King of Narnia. Edmund first begins to see the Witch's true nature as her cruelty turns toward himself. Held her

---

[4] C.S. Lewis, *The Lion, the Witch, and the Wardrobe* (New York: HarperCollins 1995), 4.
[5] Ibid., 26.
[6] Ibid., 39.
[7] Is. 14:13.

miserable prisoner, Edmund realizes that his proud fancy, fueled by the Queen's fair language, has entirely misled him. "All the things he had said to make himself believe that she was good and kind and that her side was really the right side sounded to him silly now."[8] Edmund demonstrates a truly changed heart when he tries to stop the Witch from turning the "merry party" of talking animals into stone at their Christmas feast.[9] From that moment on, when "Edmund for the first time in this story felt sorry for someone besides himself,"[10] the whole land of Narnia begins to mirror the thaw of her regent's heart.

Edmund is soon rescued in body from the White Witch, but he still must be redeemed from his guilt. The wage of treachery is death and payment for Edmund's sin must be made lest the "Deep Magic" be violated and all Narnia "be overturned and perish in fire and water."[11] As a Son of Adam and regent of the King, Edmund's guilt is intertwined with Narnia's fate. Salvation is not an individual, private matter. When Adam sinned, creation fell. If Edmund, Son of Adam is redeemed, creation will be redeemed. Instead of allowing Edmund to die for his own sin, Aslan offers himself and reveals the true character of Jupiter's joyous magnanimity. Aslan pays for Edmund's guilt with his own blood and is raised in indestructible life by the "magic deeper still" of sacrificial love, the power which turns back the disordering power of death and makes all things new.[12] By the power of Aslan's sacrifice and resurrection, the battle against the Witch will be won

---

[8] Lewis, *The Lion, the Witch, and the Wardrobe*, 114.
[9] Ibid., 115.
[10] Ibid., 117.
[11] Ibid., 142.
[12] Lewis, *The Lion*, 163.

and all four thrones at Cair Paravel will be filled. The rightful order and reign of all things in the Kingdom of Aslan is reestablished.

Saved from the Witch's Saturnocentric power, Edmund is restored to a right relationship with Aslan. In repentance and humility, Edmund becomes loyal to the rightful King of Kings and submits to Peter as the anointed High King. This submission repairs and renews his relationships with his siblings. Courageously attacking the Witch in order to break her wand, Edmund proves he is a true Jovian king of Narnia by sacrificing himself as Aslan had sacrificed for him. Full redemption then comes to all Narnia when the resurrected Aslan finally kills the White Witch and sets the children as kings and queens forever upon the four thrones of Cair Paravel. The festive, magnanimous, and chivalrous character of Jupiter rules over the coronation and all the halcyon reign of the four high regents of Narnia.[13]

While the *The Lion, the Witch, and the Wardrobe* portrays the kingdom nature of salvation, *The Voyage of the Dawn Treader* highlights its transcendent character. As the *Dawn Treader* sails east, the Narnians traverse the realm of the sun, the illuminating "eye and mind of the whole universe" and "the heaven of theologians and philosophers."[14] Sol turns sad, grey things to gleaming gold and "makes men wise and liberal."[15] Through a thousand shining details, from the gilding of the ship to the Lion's shining mane, we behold the radiance of Christ which is the light of men.

---

[13] C.S. Lewis, *The Discarded Image* (Cambridge: Cambridge University Press, 2016), 106.
[14] Ibid.
[15] Ibid.

The unenlightened Eustace is most desperately in need of a solar salvation. Eustace is a comical embodiment of the materialist worldview. No detail of his life with his parents, Harold and Alberta, admits of the spiritual realm. Eustace's darkened spirit is shriveled and immature, and the inner eye of his soul is stubbornly closed. His relationships are all utterly out of joint; he treats his parents as peers, shows no kind interest in others, has no friends, and takes no responsibility for his rude behavior, prompting the candid Reepicheep to dub him a "singularly discourteous person."[16] He mocks art and virtue, and "deep down inside him he like[s] bossing and bullying."[17] Eustace Scrub is possibly the most unenlightened, yet curiously entertaining boy one could imagine.

However, kicking and howling, Eustace is baptized violently into the spiritual realm imaginatively embodied by the wondrous world of Narnia. The first words he speaks in Narnia are those of denial: "Let me go. Let me back. I don't *like* it." "'Let you go?' said Caspian, 'But where?'"[18] After being plunged into the supernatural realm of Narnia, Eustace, the staunch materialist, frantically looks for a way out. Although the reality of this new world quickly becomes indubitable, yet Eustace persists in denying the true nature of his miraculous experiences. In anger, he demands "to be put ashore and said that at the first port he would 'lodge a disposition' against them all with the British Consul."[19] He hopes it might be a dream.[20]

---

[16] C.S. Lewis, *The Voyage of the Dawn Treader* (New York: HarperCollins, 1995), 16.
[17] Ibid., 4.
[18] Ibid., 13.
[19] Lewis, *The Voyage of the Dawn Treader*, 27.
[20] Ibid., 30.

Unable to understand the spiritual realities that give honor and strength to the Narnians, he calls "that idiot Caspian"[21] an "odious stuck-up prig."[22] Ironically, he calls Reepicheep a "little beast," but it is Eustace who usually acts as nothing more than an animated lump of cells.[23] He has a "beastly time"[24] and can hardly bear to eat the "beastly stuff" offered him on this "beastly boat."[25]

However, with "[d]ivine humility," Aslan has gently prepared Eustace for his redemption, opening "the high gates to a prodigal who is brought in kicking, struggling, resentful, and darting his eyes in every direction for a chance of escape."[26] Aslan snares Eustace with the only Solar power in which he is interested: gold. Eustace tries to take possession of the gold, but with a hardness that "is kinder than the softness of men," the darkness of Eustace's heart is brought into the light and he turns into a dragon.[27] Eustace is forced to see with his own dull eyes the dragonish stupidity of his heart. Eustace needed to experience his isolation physically in order to begin to see it spiritually. For the first time, "He began to wonder if he himself had been such a nice person as he had always supposed."[28] Prompted by the burning but golden pain of enlightenment, Eustace begins to repent; he "lifted up its voice and wept."[29] Grief broke the cold, hard, and lifeless ground of his heart so something new could grow.

---

[21] Lewis, *The Voyage of The Dawn Treader.*, 75.
[22] Ibid., 74.
[23] Ibid.
[24] Ibid., 105
[25] Ibid., 71.
[26] C.S. Lewis, *Surprised by Joy*, In *The Inspirational Writings of C.S. Lewis* (New York: Inspirational Press, 1994), 125.
[27] Ibid.
[28] Lewis, *The Voyage of The Dawn Treader*, 92.
[29] Ibid..

Now acknowledging his own soul, Eustace is able to connect with other souls at last, and his relationships begin to heal. As "enormous and boiling tears… flowed from his eyes," Eustace is literally turned inside out and others are, for the first time, allowed to see his real self.[30] Queen Lucy the Valiant kisses his scaly face and the others all encourage him with their friendship. Eustace begins to function spiritually. He finally perceives the needs of others and becomes helpful. He discovers "the pleasure (quite new to him) of being liked and, still more, of liking other people."[31] His greatest adversary, Reepicheep, becomes "his most constant comforter."[32]

Eustace is now awake but not yet fully redeemed. The darkness of his heart has been exposed and his soul has been softened but Aslan, sun-god, and "killer of dragons" must come with his solar light to finally dispel the darkness which entombs Eustace still.[33] Aslan kills the dragon of sin and sets the boy free. Eustace dies to his old self as "the very first tear [Aslan] made was so deep that I thought it had gone right into my heart,"[34] but then he is raised into new spiritual life, "smooth and soft."[35] Eustace is baptized by his Priest and King and drawn into the light of life itself.

Aslan does not ever speak aloud to Eustace, for he would teach him how to be illumined by God from within in order to live spiritually from the inside out. Although Eustace is still tempted to question its reality, and wonders aloud to Edmund if it "may have been all a dream," his life

---

[30] Lewis, *The Voyage of The Dawn Treader*, 100
[31] Ibid, 102.
[32] Ibid., 103.
[33] Michael Ward, *Planet Narnia: The Seven Heavens in the Imagination of C.S. Lewis* (Oxford: Oxford University Press, 2010), 113.
[34] Lewis, *The Voyage of The Dawn Treader*, 109.
[35] Ibid., 109.

has become permeable to the spiritual realm.[36] He is open to Edmund's exhortation and he laughs and wonders at his new miraculous clothes. Most importantly, the redeemed Eustace takes responsibility for his own soul and apologizes to Edmund.

Furthermore, as it does in all the Chronicles, salvation also brings redemption to Eustace's relationships. He now lives in a right relationship with Aslan, who is no longer to him the hated enemy but now the Light of his world. His relationship with his cousins, Caspian, and all the Narnians is made new. There was a "great ... rejoicing when Edmund and the restored Eustace walked into the breakfast circle round the camp fire."[37] Enlightenment has even restored Eustace's relationship to the material realm. Eustace admits to Edmund, "You'd think me simply phony if I told you how I felt about my own arms."[38] He no longer sees his own body as *just* a bundle of nerves and molecules, but rather as a wondrous, holy gift.

If we could take the time to examine them one-by-one, we would see that all *The Chronicles of Narnia* are saturated with the glory of redemption. Each story is composed in harmony with the Great Story, wherein all things are redeemed and brought back into right relationship, all with all, and all part of "the majestic order that runs through all things."[39] Lewis believed that the intricate and ordered dance of the planetary spheres in the old medieval model of the cosmos imaginatively embodied the harmonious, unified grandeur of the Gospel, and he delighted in its "combined splendor,

---

[36] Lewis, *The Voyage of The Dawn Treader*, 106.
[37] Ibid., 111.
[38] Ibid., 109.
[39] Ward, *Planet Narnia*, 252.

sobriety, and coherence."[40] By coloring each of his Chronicles with a different planetary atmosphere, Lewis artistically reflects this old vision of cosmic grandeur and reveals different aspects of what it means for our many stories to be shaped and transformed by Christ's one salvation story. As we gaze into Narnia, through its varying planetary lenses, we can begin to see how the salvation of each saint and every kingdom is woven together in a glorious, multifaceted pattern of cosmic restoration.

Most often we cannot pinpoint the exact moment we too stepped through the Wardrobe or fell through a painting and into this great cosmic story ourselves. If we consider a specific minute we bowed our knees before God or the moment we were baptized before his people, "it would be nice, and fairly nearly true, to say that," like Eustace, we were "from that time forth" utterly new creatures. However, "to be strictly accurate," we must confess that this side of eternity, we too have only begun to be different. But oh, joy! The great cure *has* begun.[41]

---

[40] Lewis, *The Discarded Image*, 216.
[41] Lewis, *The Voyage of The Dawn Treader*, 112.

The Response

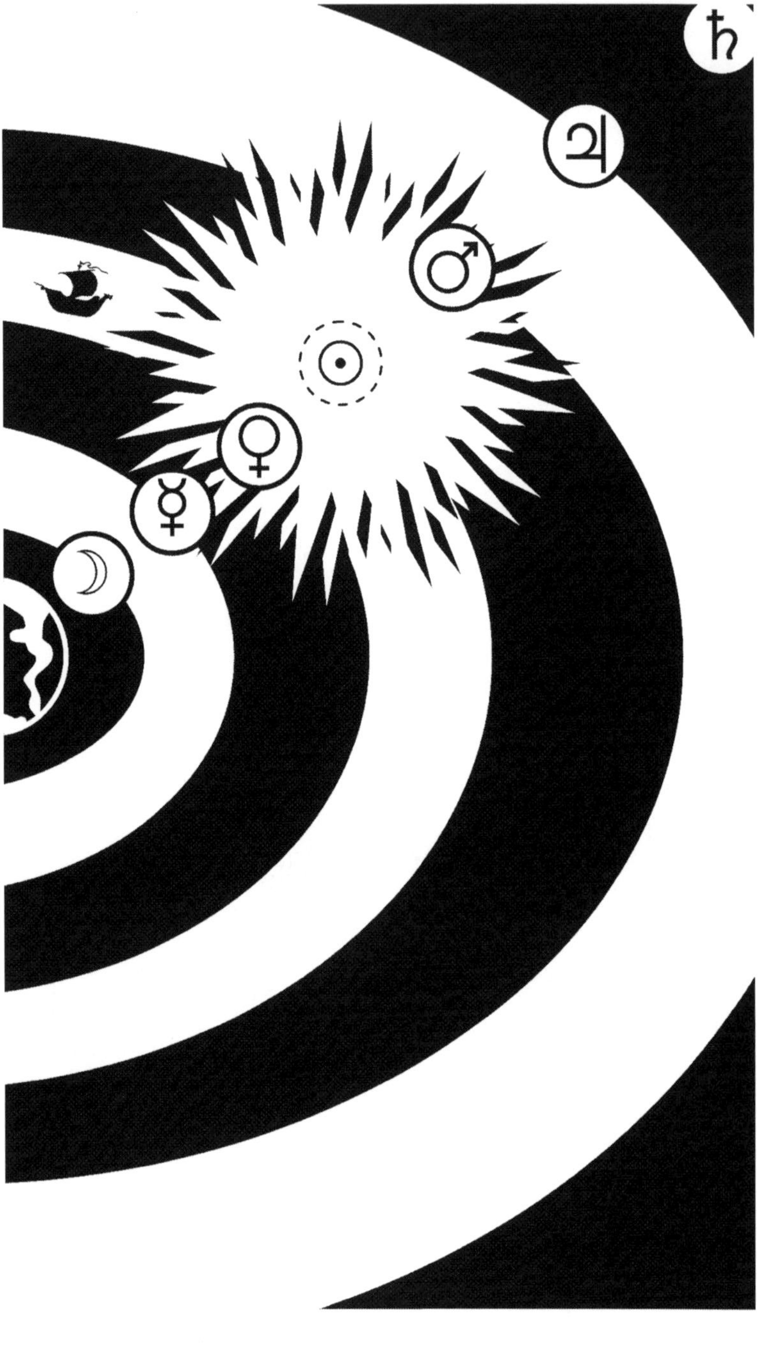

The Voyage of the Dawn Treader and the Rehabilitation of Practical Reason

Jason Monroe

"We must extend the word Reason to include what our ancestors called Practical Reason and confess that judgements such as society ought to be preserved . . . are not mere sentiments but are rationality itself. . ." C.S. Lewis, *The Abolition of Man*

Imagine strolling downtown and asking passersby, "How would you define reasonable action?" The result will likely be many different accounts. One may run, "Scientifically-proven progress is reasonable." "Progress" here is vague; nevertheless, this view emphasizes the forward march of humankind — possibly at any cost — following the philosophies of scientists. For science, if more than a methodology, must be the collection of professionals implementing its methods. A second claim might be, "It is doing what I feel is best." Again, "best" needs defining, but this point posits personal feeling and desire as the basis of reason. Thirdly, there is the deference of the honest follower: "Our leaders know what is reasonable." Leaders are often advantaged in many ways, but are they wiser? To assume so accepts Nietzschean power philosophy. This is popular, but also thought to be domineering and unsympathetic; after all, leaders can be wrong and cruel.

A fourth option is to associate reasonable action with Practical Reason — "the employment of reason in service of living a good life."[1] C.S. Lewis says that "our duty to do good to all men is an axiom of Practical Reason."[2] Distinct from Pure Reason, the faculty that does a math sum or recognizes, *a priori*, that bachelors are unmarried, Practical Reason is the association of reason with good behavior. If reason inherently includes a moral component, it will not so easily become subordinated to whim, pride, or cold calculation.

One may study detachedly the general trend of Practical Reason throughout the ages and attempt to live it out. But stories with compelling examples of living well will always be necessary for character formation. Lewis's *The Voyage of the Dawn Treader* so happens to be one of these very tales. Below, we will look at how this story can help the realization, "what is reasonable is also what is good," dawn in the mind.

---

[1] Christopher Toner, "Medieval Theories of Practical Reason," *The Internet Encyclopedia of Philosophy*, accessed November 28, 2018, https://www.iep.utm.edu/prac-med.

[2] C.S. Lewis, *The Abolition of Man*, in *The Essential C.S. Lewis*, ed. Lyle W. Dorsett (New York: Simon & Schuster, Inc., 1988), 445.

In *Planet Narnia*, Michael Ward chooses a Lewisian term which is helpful to our discussion. Lewis was fond of Donegal, Ireland, all his life,[3] so Ward deems *donegality* appropriate for "the spiritual essence or quiddity of a work of art as intended by the artist and inhabited unconsciously by the reader."[4] He includes some of Lewis's stabs at defining it as a story's "peculiar unity of effect produced by a special balancing and patterning of thoughts and classes of thoughts'; 'a state or quality'; 'flavour or atmosphere'; 'smell or taste'; 'mood'; 'quiddity.'"[5] A story's donegality is no one element: it is the whole aesthetic gestalt experienced by the reader. It is more than the sum of its parts. A great symphony may move one to tears, but only as the complete symphony. If isolated from the whole, the movements, rhythms, and melodies would not produce the same effect.

Donegality is important to consider because Ward argues that *VDT*'s donegality is solar through and through. The imagery and symbolism of *VDT* create an atmosphere powerfully redolent of Sol (the sun). Ward says *VDT* has "indeed the most obvious of the seven Narnian donegalities:"[6] the book's title nods to the sun's rising — the dawn; the ship sails ever Eastward toward an increasingly large sun; and Caspian partakes of water which is like "drinkable light."[7] Similar instances of solar imagery abound. Ward's point is that the drenching of the story in sun-symbolism is meant to convey themes

---

[3] Michael Ward, *Planet Narnia* (New York: Oxford Unversity Press, 2008), 75.
[4] Ibid., 75.
[5] Ibid., 16.
[6] Ibid., 108.
[7] C.S. Lewis, *The Voyage of the Dawn Treader*, in *The Chronicles of Narnia* (New York: Harper Collins, 1998), 532.

traditionally associated with the personality of Sol. One of these themes is the proper use of reason. Lewis's poem, "The Planets" is a brief summary of the archetypal characteristics of the planets. Upon reaching Sol's sphere, we discover:

> When his arrow glances
> Through mortal mind, mists are parted
> And mild as morning the mellow wisdom
> Breathes o'er the breast, broadening eastward
> Clear and cloudless.[8]

Largely, Sol's influence yields illumination, clearing up mental confusion ("mists are parted"), and nurturing an ordinate use of reason ("mellow wisdom"). Therefore, *VDT*, baptized imaginatively in Sol's rays, can encourage a life lived according to Practical Reason, which contrasts with the above three rival conceptions of reason.

The first, scientism — the view that the scientific method takes precedence in all pursuits of truth — is parodied in Eustace Scrubb, whom Doris Myers appropriately calls a "Boy without a Chest."[9] His education has been purely modern given he "had read none of the right books."[10] "He liked books if they were books of information and had pictures of grain elevators or of fat foreign children doing exercises in model schools."[11] These books "had a lot to say about exports and imports and governments and drains, but they were weak on dragons."[12] One of his diary entries expresses

---

[8] C.S. Lewis, *Poems*, ed. Walter Hooper (Orlando: Mariner, 1992), 13.

[9] Doris T. Myers, *C.S. Lewis in Context* (Kent: Kent State University Press, 1944), 145. The reference is to Lewis's *The Abolition of Man*, where "Men Without Chests" are those untrained in virtuous habits.

[10] Lewis, *The Voyage of the Dawn Treader*, 463.

[11] Ibid., 425.

[12] Ibid.

detestation at the ship's "primitive indoors" and complains of "no proper saloon, no radio, no bathrooms, no deck-chairs."[13] Eustace's wholly modern education values hyper-sanitized social conditions and pragmatic policy over authentic community. Trusting science and technology over Practical Reason informs and stimulates Eustace's uninspired outlook.

His early discontent with the crew reveals a clash of worldviews. The excitement of the *Dawn Treader*'s crew relies mostly on their bare experiences upon the waves at nature's mercy. They are more open than Eustace to the awe and wonder evoked by a closer connection with Creation. No 21st-century advancements are necessary for adventure when one may encounter the supernatural at every turn. Crucial for the crew is their spirits oriented toward a worthwhile goal — in this case, that of finding the seven lost Narnian lords. Splashing in the shallows of a modern outlook, Eustace is blind to the mystery of the transcendent, and he becomes upset. To calm his soul's tempest, he must acquiesce to growing and maturing with the ship's crew so as to learn (even if the hard way) the lessons he could have learned more easily by reading good fairy tales.

Although Eustace has allowed scientism to sculpt his sentiments, his hostility toward the *Dawn Treader*'s milieu begins to cool as he increasingly adheres to Practical Reason. An understanding of charity is integral to his transformation. He begins to serve his shipmates and is less self-absorbed: his temporary exile into dragonhood becomes, in St. Paul's words, "a thorn in the flesh,"

---

[13] Lewis, *The Voyage of The Dawn Treader.*, 464.

spurring him on to good deeds.[14] He flies over the island, procuring "provisions for the ship;" he was "anxious to help"; and "he was a very humane killer" of animals for food.[15] As befits Sol, Lewis's language grows clearer as he describes Eustace's moral alteration: "It would be nice, and fairly true, to say that 'from that time forth Eustace was a different boy.' To be strictly accurate, he began to be a different boy."[16]

Another *Dawn Treader* voyager, Lucy, is also tempted by a scientistic view of the world when the magician's book presents her with the opportunity to utilize magic to achieve her own ends. A particular incantation can make her beautiful "*beyond the lot of mortals*,"[17] but she resists with Aslan's help. Myers explains that "Lucy models the practice of proper restraints on magic (or, by extension, the near-magic powers of science and technology)."[18] Lewis thought that science and magic, in a sense, were twins: they both offer open avenues toward inordinate control over nature and other men.[19] Thus Lucy's resistance to magic's allure aptly parallels a wise resistance to the glittering promises of scientific progress. When wielded by fallen human nature, some scientific powers possess a dangerously high potential for more harm than good. Commenting on the scientism of modern culture, John West writes, "In the age of science, almost anything can be taken seriously, if only it is defended in the name of

---

[14] 2 Cor. 12:7, NABRE.
[15] Lewis, *The Voyage of the Dawn Treader*, 471.
[16] Ibid., 476.
[17] Ibid., 495.
[18] Myers, *C.S. Lewis in Context*, 144.
[19] Lewis, *The Abolition of Man*, 457.

science."[20] However, the indispensable realm of "ought" is what Lucy wisely concedes to. Being, as the Zaleskis put it, an "ideal of faithful reason,"[21] Lucy understands that possession of power does not automatically justify its arbitrary use.

The second claim mentioned above comes from the proponents of personal feeling and offers another bid for reason's hand. From a bird's-eye view, the *Dawn Treader*'s voyage is a metaphor for putting reason before appetites: waves are often a symbol of man's tumultuous passions, and to be overcome by them is to relinquish reason's control. In contrast, the crew stays their course, regardless of storms or difficulties. Reepicheep is probably the best example, given his inexorable march toward Aslan's country. His resolve is such that no circumstance will persuade him to abandon his principles. Determined to "sink with my nose to the sunrise,"[22] he exemplifies a rational pursuit, unhindered by whim. In the ship that is someone's soul, often desire dawdles to submit to reason's rudder; but with hard work, feelings will come around to follow eventually. Reepicheep's pure conscience and clear aims have solidified into a disposition as consistent as the rising sun. Further, his matured virtue allows his wisdom to overflow encouragingly into Eustace, who found it "very dreary being a dragon."[23]

Practical Reason is also featured in Edmund's shrewd investigation at the pool on Deathwater Island. Ward

---

[20] John West, "The Magician's Twin," in *The Magician's Twin: C.S. Lewis on Science, Scientism, and Society*, ed. John West (Seattle: Discovery Institute Press, 2012), 24.
[21] Philip Zaleski and Carol Zaleski, *The Fellowship: The Literary Lives of the Inklings* (New York: Farrar, Straus and Giroux, 2015), 387.
[22] Lewis, *The Voyage of the Dawn Treader*, 524.
[23] Ibid., 471.

points out that Peter's knightliness is emphasized in *Prince Caspian* to suit the tale's martial donegality.[24] The same principle works under Sol's influence, where Edmund, "the only one of the party who had read several detective stories,"[25] displays clear, objective thought over emotion. Reason is critical to detective work, which includes intense investigation and detached application of logic. By process of elimination, Edmund rules out possible fates for the owner of a solitary suit of armor. His helpful analysis at the pool with the Midas Touch counters Reepicheep's impulsive suggestion to dive in and prevents him and the others from unwittingly becoming forever-submerged, golden statues.[26]

Our third substitute for Practical Reason is authority *per se*. Not uncommonly, citizens trust the judgment of their presidents, prime ministers, or kings simply by virtue of their offices. Everyone trusts authority of some sort, so it is pivotal to clarify that the *ad verecundiam* fallacy indicates an improper or unjustified authority. Recall, in *VDT*, the vexingly repetitious replies of the Dufflepuds on the Island of the Voices. Myers notes, "Their constant rejection of their natural lord, Coriakin, does not free them; instead, it puts them completely under the power of the Chief."[27] The Dufflepuds think it is reasonable to follow a rogue authority credulously and completely. Good authority, for example, does not seek to control minds, but encourages free thinking. Conversely, by following an inferior authority, the Dufflepuds virtually have lost all their independent thought. They now only parrot their leader or

---

[24] Ward, *Planet Narnia*, 96.
[25] Lewis, *The Voyage of the Dawn Treader*, 482.
[26] Ibid., 482-483.
[27] Myers, *C.S. Lewis in Context*, 144.

repeat misled maxims: "That's our chief. You can depend on what he says. He's telling you the truth, he is," and "Keep it up, Chief . . . You're talking like a book."[28]

By snubbing their true authority, they forfeit authentic freedom and succumb to fear. The Dufflepuds are so mortified by Coriakin that they force Lucy to approach the magic book for them and remove the invisibility spell. They resemble the youngsters in Chesterton's *Orthodoxy* who huddle together in fear, bereft of rules:

> Christianity is the only frame which has preserved the pleasure of Paganism. We might fancy some children playing on the flat grassy top of some tall island in the sea. So long as there was a wall round the cliff's edge they could fling themselves into every frantic game and make the place the noisiest of nurseries. But the walls were knocked down, leaving the naked peril of the precipice. They did not fall over; but when their friends returned to them they were all huddled in terror in the centre of the island; and their song had ceased.[29]

Legitimate liberty requires law derived from Practical Reason. As with Chesterton's analogy, if moral boundaries keep moving, or disappear altogether, fear easily becomes predominant. This causes hesitancy and eventually paralysis of will and action. However, when moral boundaries are firmly established in one's life, virtue can blossom, roam free, and become habit. Awareness of a boundary causes confidence in planning and moving within it, which is a necessary component to human flourishing.

We see authority adhering to Practical Reason when King Caspian demotes Gumpas, the governor of the Lone

---

[28] Lewis, *The Voyage of the Dawn Treader*, 488.
[29] G.K. Chesterton, *Orthodoxy* (New York: Image Books, 2014), chp. 9, iBooks.

Islands. Gumpas has become a paper-pusher who indifferently maintains either unjust practices (slavery) or lazy apathies (failures to pay taxes).[30] Gumpas, immersed in facts and figures, puts materials before men. By withholding tribute, he has severed himself from Caspian, whose rule is legitimate since it follows natural law and is appointed by Aslan. Caspian is a virtuous leader, and his kingship "contrasts the bureaucratic justice of our modern world with the justice of the king under the law."[31] Rightful royal offices play an important role from the beginning to the end of Narnia's timeline. The Great Lion anoints Frank and Helen as the first "King and Queen of Narnia, father and mother of many kings that shall be."[32] The divine line persists through Tirion, the "last of the Kings of Narnia,"[33] and even in the golden-gated garden in *The Last Battle*, the kings and queens retain their regal titles.[34] Due to the nature of Caspian's appointment and policy, his deposition of Gumpas is a proper application Practical Reason.

Lewis argues that the majority of people in ages past have intuited Practical Reason. A healthy conscience will prompt voluntary submission to good authorities. Throughout history, authority is thought to be an irremovable, essential element of human society. Eradicating it would be akin to removing someone's brain and expecting him to function properly. One need not scour obscure (or even only Christian) sources to find support for rightful rule. Lewis quotes Plato,

---

[30] Lewis, *The Voyage of the Dawn Treader*, 449.
[31] Myers, *C.S. Lewis in Context*, 143.
[32] Lewis, *The Magician's Nephew*, in *The Chronicles of Narnia*, 699.
[33] Ibid., 675.
[34] Ibid., 764.

> Has it escaped you that, in the eyes of gods and good men, your native land deserves from you more honour, worship, and reverence than your mother and father and all your ancestors? That you should give a softer answer to its anger than to a father's anger? That if you cannot persuade it to alter its mind you must obey it in all quietness, whether it binds you or beats you or sends you to a war where you may get wounds or death?[35]

The *Dawn Treader* crew are not merely following their passions, gallivanting on the open seas, and labeling it true liberty. They are questing under a formal authority, which, when taken seriously, becomes — paradoxically — the most free and jovial of enterprises. The crew's joy stems from following good authority, built on Practical Reason, which is indispensable to their unity and common good.

VDT is a sunny homage to the best way to live, and it provides a shining, lighthearted, hopeful solution to the dead-end alternatives mentioned above. A bearing directed by scientism, whim, or illegitimate authority will inevitably drift into injustice. Reasonable action, if it is to be consistent *and* good, must be grounded in Practical Reason. *VDT* does not stop at adventure, but satisfies the imaginative hunger produced by reason in the wrong place. The story can be viewed as an guide for undergoing spiritual struggles and emerging victorious since it is, in a way, a call to action which requires reliance on a standard. The sailors must employ Practical Reason or the vessel's prow will flounder in its progress toward the peace of the lily-covered Silver Sea and the joy of Aslan's country. Like physical or moral dangers in one's life, any perils en route could have spelled disaster for the crew. But the compass

---

[35] Lewis, *The Abolition of Man*, 461.

was never neglected, the right path not rejected. Therefore, when this Sol-centered tale seemed at its darkest, light conquered fear in the form of an albatross that "offered good guidance" to Drinian and comforted Lucy with, "Courage, dear heart."[36]

---

[36] Lewis, *The Voyage of the Dawn Treader*, 511.

By Jove!

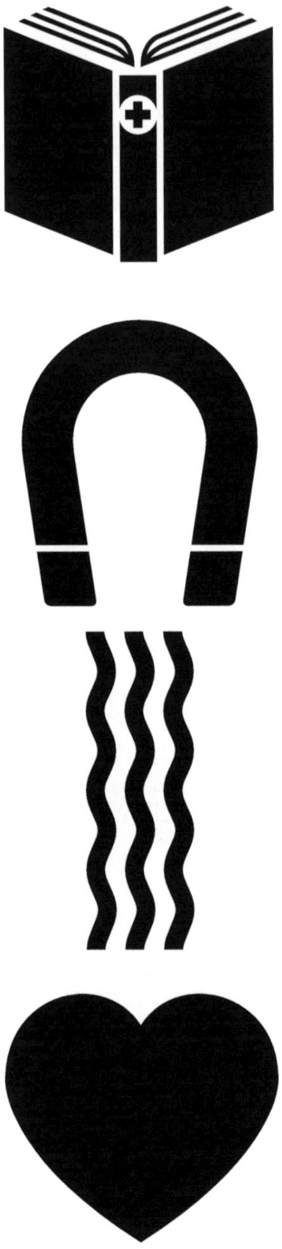

Gravitational Pull

Marshall Arthur Liszt

Something pulled you, compelled you, made you pick this up instead of something else. You were driven to do it. You chose to do it. Or you didn't choose and instead it chose you. We could quibble about the way to express this all day, but the fact remains: along *this* particular timeline, in *this* possible world, right *this* moment — <u>you</u> are reading a journal of imaginative apologetics, and not doing otherwise.

We all have a working knowledge of gravity by what it does. Physicists can express facts about gravity using various formulae, but even without such mathematical language we all live our lives in ways that conform to this very real, ubiquitous phenomenon.

Juxtapose those two thoughts for a moment: that life, when considered personally, is like a story, and that certain phenomena (like gravity) exert a pervasive, invisible influence on the way we live our lives.

… could it be that <u>yours</u> is a story where the subject is being pulled ever closer into orbit around something massively important? What could be so powerful — like gravity — that it would bend a person's timeline so?

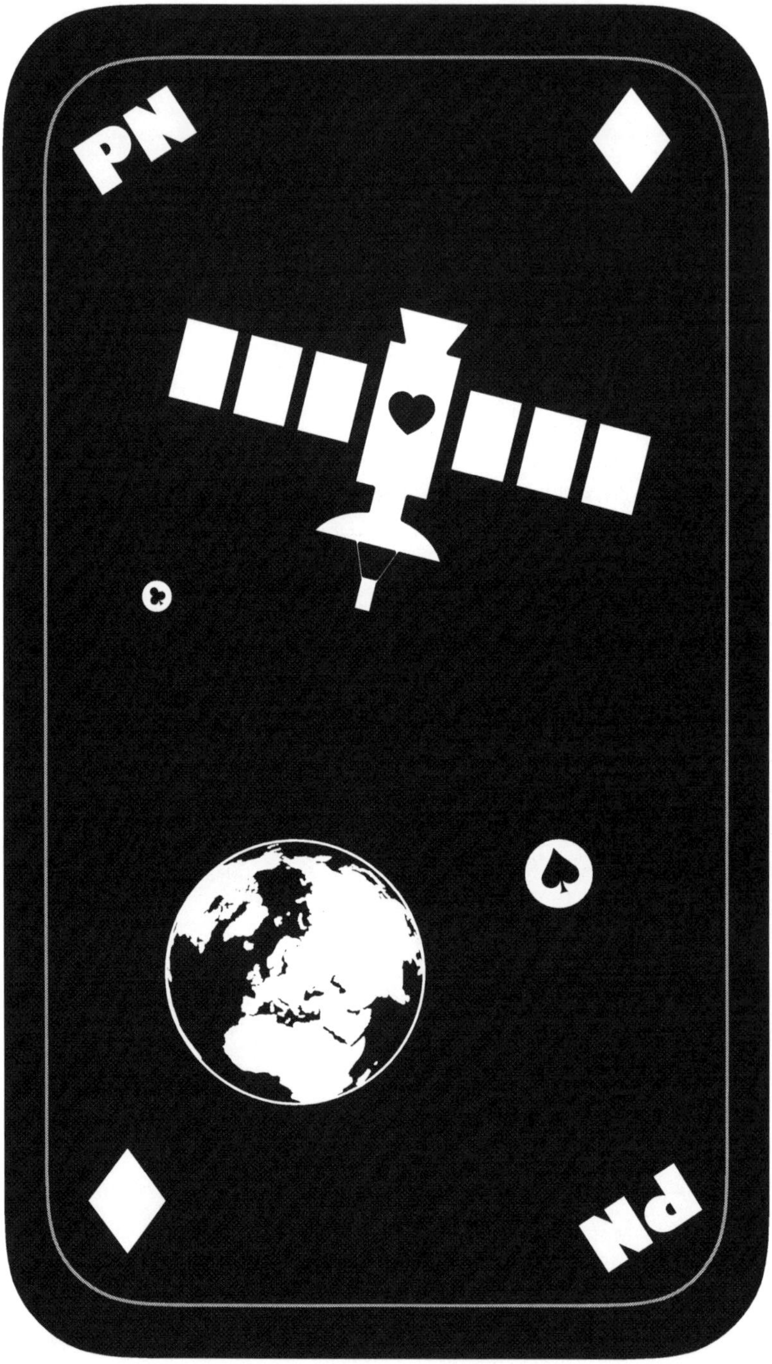
PN
PN

Quarantine

Adam L. Brackin

The traveler's wife had never known true fear and loneliness until her husband went down to the quarantine world. Their whole adult lives Ayda had shared her thoughts and feelings with Mev thanks to the LOGOS uplink on the vessel they called home. Normally the link was preserved during a walk, and she joined his mind on these alien planets, but something this time had gone very differently, and the link had been severed.

So, when Mev finally returned to her, ragged in body and mind and teetering on the verge of collapse; Ayda caught him, embraced him, and kissed him, relishing the intimate blending of their minds once more, and feeling him do the same. They held each other for a long time, until both had cried tears of joy and relief.

"*I wanted to return when I realized I was alone,*" he assured her, "*but I knew that if I did, you would never let me go back down again.*" Both instantly knew that he was right.

"What did you find?" With a jolt, Ayda felt Mev push her out of his mind. It scared her more than when she had been alone, until she realized it scared him too.

"*I know why this world is forbidden, Ayda.*"

Slowly, Mev opened his mind and showed her a sequence of wonderful and terrifying things he had seen. Memories of ruined cities, forests, and a moon in shadow came to her. Great river valleys of rusting machines and crumbling walls. And then she stood in a great stone building filled with strange rectangular objects.

"What are they?"

"*They are called books. I looked at them until I could read, but I did not fully understand them.*"

"How is that possible? All knowledge is good."

Suddenly, Mev closed himself off again. "*Not all. I found writings both powerful and terrible, and some full of dysfunction, disobedience, and wickedness, but also ones filled with love, and goodness, and truth.*" Ayda joined in his memory of the books, and ideas and words that she had never considered filled her mind. An overwhelming deluge of light swept through her very soul, and she glimpsed a darkness she had no name for.

This time it was Ayda who pulled away from Mev in horror, scrambling to her feet. Never had she known ideas like these. But Mev was not showing her mere silly abstract imaginings. He was remembering things he had read while on that quarantined world. In her core, Ayda knew it was all real. The forbidden world had put fear and anger into the mind of Mev. He was contaminated. And now she was *afraid* of her husband. *How could that even be*?

But Mev didn't stop there. He began sharing more ideas with her that were impossible. Creatures killing one another. Beings covering their form with cloth. Misusing one-another's bodies for personal pleasure. Speaking untrue words for selfish gain.

With revulsion, Ayda realized she was contaminated too. She screamed.

And with that, the wall that Mev had been keeping everything else behind crumbled. Ayda saw that Mev's decision to return to the ship had been the most difficult thing he'd ever done. He'd known it would change them. Mev had understood the purpose of the quarantine much too late.

"The infection is a kind of knowledge unto itself, Ayda. Not of goodness and truth — for all beings are born with that — but of dysfunction, corruption, and error."

To glance at it even once was to be contaminated by it. And with that, she knew. The error had set up in their hearts long before Mev had ever stepped into that world. The moment they had decided to disobey LOGOS and ignore the quarantine, they had become contaminated too.

They clutched each other and sobbed. The link was already fading. They could never leave that quarantined world now. They would go down together now and start a different kind of life.

Somewhere warm and beautiful, she hoped.

Mev stared at her awkwardly. Ayda realized she was covering herself with her hands and so looked away from him in shame. He turned away too. There was a time when that idea would have been fascinating to them both, but for some reason she couldn't seem to remember why anymore.

"Are we naked?" she asked. Though of course, she already knew the answer.

Bibliography

Seven Questions:

Lewis, C. S. "On Obstinacy in Belief." *The Sewanee Review*. Accessed December 3, 2018. https://thesewaneereview.com/on-obstinacy-and-belief/.

MacDonald, George. *Phantastes, A Faerie Romance*. Grand Rapids, MI: Eerdmans, 2000.

O'Fee, James. "Melchizedek and Jupiter, by James O'Fee." Impala Publications. January 1, 2009. Accessed December 3, 2018. http://www.impalapublications.com/blog/index.php?/archives/3458-Melchizedek-and-Jupiter,-8by-James-OFee.html.

"Online Articles." The Marion E. Wade Center at Wheaton College. Accessed December 3, 2018. https://www.wheaton.edu/academics/academic-centers/wadecenter/publications/vii-journal/contents/online-articles/.

Ward, Michael. *Planet Narnia*. New York: Oxford University Press, 2008.

Where Paradoxes Play

Bernstein, Richard. *Beyond Objectivism and Relativism: Science, Hermeneutics, and Praxis*. Philadelphia: University of Pennsylvania Press, 1983.

Gableman, Josephine. *A Theology of Nonsense*. Eugene, Oregon: Pickwick Publications, 2016.

Lewis, C. S. *George MacDonald: An Anthology of 365 Readings*. London: Collins, 2016.

--------. *The Screwtape Letters*. New York: HarperCollins, 1996.

Quash, Ben and Michael Ward, eds. *Heresies and How to Avoid Them: Why it Matters what Christians Believe*. London: SPCK, 2007.

Tillich, Paul. *Dynamics of Faith*. New York: Harper One, 1957.

Why We Love to Visit Narnia

Lewis, C. S. *The Chronicles of Narnia*. New York: HarperCollins, 2001.

(Re)Considering the Planet Narnia Thesis

Dickieson, Brenton. "A New C.S. Lewis Letter with Details About Narnia." A Pilgrim in Narnia September 12, 2018. Accessed November 20, 2018. https://apilgriminnarnia.com/2018/09/12/new-lewisletter/.

--------. "'Die Before You Die': St. Paul's Cruciformity in C.S. Lewis." In *Both Sides of the Wardrobe: C.S. Lewis, Theological Imagination and Everyday Discipleship*. Edited by Rob Fennell. Eugene, OR: Wipf & Stock, 2015.

Hooper, Walter ed. *The Collected Letters of C.S. Lewis: Vol. 3: Narnia, Cambridge, and Joy 1950-1963*. New York: HarperSanFrancisco, 2007.

Huttar, Charles A. "C.S. Lewis's Narnia and the 'Grand Design.'" In *The Long for a Form: Essays on the Fiction of C.S. Lewis*. Edited by Peter J. Schakel. Kent, OH: Kent State University Press, 1977.

Lewis, C. S. *An Experiment in Criticism*. Cambridge: Canto Classics, 2012.

--------. *Letters to Malcolm: Chiefly on Prayer*. London: Goeffrey Bles, 1964.

--------. "The Alliterative Metre." In *Selected Literary Essays*. Edited by Walter Hooper. Cambridge: Canto Classics, 2013.

--------. *The Discarded Image: An Introduction to Medieval and Renaissance Literature*. Cambridge: Canto Classics, 1994.

Lewis, C.S. and E.M.W. Tillyard. *The Personal Heresy: A Controversy*. New York: HarperOne, 1939.

Vaus, Will. *The Hidden Story of Narnia: A Book-by-Book Guide to C.S. Lewis's Spiritual Themes*. Cheshire, CT: Winged Lion Press, 2010.

Ward, Michael. Introduction to a new audio course. "Christology, Cosmology, and C.S. Lewis." Now You Know Media Inc., 2017.

--------. *Planet Narnia*. New York: Oxford University Press, 2008.

A Defense of Planet Narnia

Barrett, Justin. "Some Planets in Narnia: A Quantitative Investigation of the Planet Narnia Thesis." *VII* 27 (January 2010). Accessed December 3, 2018. https://www.wheaton.edu/media/migrated-images-amp-files/media/files/centers-and-institutes/wade-center/Barrett_Narnia_web.pdf.

Brown, Devin. "Planet Narnia Spin, Spun Out." CSLewis.com. May 13, 2009. Accessed December 3, 2018. http:// www.cslewis.com/planet-narnia-spin-spun-out/.

Ward, Michael. *Planet Narnia*. New York: Oxford University Press, 2008.

--------. "Quality not Quantity" *VII* Vol 28 (2012). Accessed December 3, 2018. https://www.wheaton.edu/media/migrated-images-amp-files/media/files/centers-and-institutes/wade-center/vii/vii20online20articles/Ward_QualityorQuantity2.pdf.

Return to Planet Narnia

Beaumont, Francis. *The Knight of the Burning Pestle*. First performed in 1607.

Chaucer, Geoffrey. *The Canterbury Tales*.

Dickens, Charles. *Little Dorrit*.

English Literature in the Sixteenth Century Excluding Drama. Oxford: Clarendon Press, 1954.

Ford, Paul F. *Companion to Narnia*. New York: HarperCollins, 2005.

Herodotus, *The Histories*.

Lewis, C. S. "A Note on Comus," *Studies in Medieval and Renaissance Literature*.

--------. *Image and Imagination*. Cambridge: Cambridge University Press, 2013.

--------. *Miracles: A Preliminary Study*. Glasgow: Collins, 1980.

--------. *Perelandra*. New York: HarperCollins, 2012.

--------. *Poems*. New York: Harvest, 1992.

--------. *The Chronicles of Narnia*. New York: HarperCollins, 2001.

--------. *The Discarded Image: An Introduction to Medieval and Renaissance Literature*. Cambridge: Canto Classics, 1994.

--------. "The 'Morte Darthur.'" In *Studies in Medieval and Renaissance Literature*. Edited by Walter Hooper. Cambridge: Cambridge University Press, 1966.

Malory, Thomas. *Le Morte Darthur*. Oxford: Oxford University Press, 1998.

Pliny the Elder. *Natural History*. Translated by W. H. S. Jones. Cambridge, MA: Harvard University Press, 1949-54.

Roberts, Edward A. ed. *A Comprehensive Etymological Dictionary of the Spanish Language with Families of Words 20 Based on Indo-European Roots, Vol. I (A-G)*. Bloomington, IN: XLibris, 2014.

Ward, Michael. *Planet Narnia*. New York: Oxford University Press, 2008.

Yandell, Stephen. "The Allegory of Love and The Discarded Image: C.S. Lewis as Medievalist." In *C. S. Lewis: Life, Works, and Legacy, Vol. 4: Scholar, Teacher, and Public Intellectual*. Edited by Bruce L. Edwards. Santa Barbara, CA: Praeger, 2007.

Table Narnia

Brown, Devin. *Inside Narnia: A Guide to Exploring The Lion, the Witch and the Wardrobe*. Grand Rapids: Baker, 2005.

Duriez, Colin. *A Field Guide to Narnia*. Downers Grove, IL: InterVarsity Press, 2004.

Ford, Paul F. *Companion to Narnia*. San Francisco: HarperSanFrancisco, 1994.

Guerber, H. A. *Myths of the Norsemen: From the Eddas and Sagas*. London: George C. Harrap, 1908.

Lewis, C.S. "Miracles." In *God in the Dock*. Grand Rapids, MI: Wm. B. Eerdmans, 2014.

--------. *Prince Caspian*. New York: Harper, 1980.

--------. *The C. S. Lewis Bible*. New York: HarperCollins, 2010.

--------. *The Collected Letters of C.S. Lewis Volume I: Family Letters 1905-1931*. New York: Harper, 2004.

--------. *The Lion, the Witch, and the Wardrobe*. New York: Harper, 1980.

--------. *The Voyage of the Dawn Treader*. New York: Harper, 1980.

Otto, Rudolph. *The Idea of the Holy*. New York: Penguin, 1959.

Sheldrake, Philip. *Living Between Worlds: Place and Journey in Celtic Spirituality*. Cambridge, MA: Cowley Publications, 1995.

Underhill, Evelyn. "Mysticism." Christian Classics Ethereal Library. Accessed October 17, 2018. Http://www.ccel.org/ccel/underhill/mysticism.pdf?membership_type=b10f8d8331236b8b61aa39bc6f86075c12d7e005.

Vaus, Will. "Lewis and Stonehenge." *The Official Website of C.S. Lewis*. October 17, 2018. Accessed December 3, 2018. http://www.cslewis.com/lewis-and-stonehenge/.

Ward, Michael. *Planet Narnia*. New York: Oxford University Press, 2008.

Yuasa, Kyoko. *C. S. Lewis and Christian Postmodernism: Word, Image, and Beyond*. Eugene: Wipf and Stock, 2016.

The Cure Has Begun

Lewis, C. S. *Poems*. New York: Harvest, 1992.

--------. "Surprised by Joy." In *The Inspirational Writings of C.S. Lewis*. New York: Inspirational Press, 1994.

--------. *The Discarded Image*. Cambridge: Cambridge University Press, 2016.

--------. *The Lion, the Witch, and the Wardrobe*. New York: HarperCollins, 1995.

--------. *The Voyage of the Dawn Treader*. New York: HarperCollins, 1995.

Ward, Michael. *Planet Narnia*. New York: Oxford University Press, 2008.

VDT and the Rehabilitation of Practical Reason

Chesterton, G.K. *Orthodoxy*. New York: Image Books, 2014. iBooks.

Lewis, C.S. *The Abolition of Man*, in *The Essential C.S. Lewis*. Edited by Lyle W. Dorsett. New York: Simon & Schuster, Inc., 1988.

--------. *The Chronicles of Narnia*. New York: Harper Collins, 1998.

--------. *Poems*. Edited by Walter Hooper. Orlando: Mariner, 1992.

Myers, Doris T. *C.S. Lewis in Context*. Kent: KSU Press, 1994.

Toner, Christopher. "Medieval Theories of Practical Reason." *The Internet Encyclopedia of Philosophy*. Accessed November 28, 2018. https://www.iep.utm.edu/prac-med.

Ward, Michael. *Planet Narnia*. New York: Oxford University Press, 2008.

West, John G. "The Magician's Twin," in *The Magician's Twin*. Edited by John G. West. Seattle: Discovery Institute Press, 2012.

Zaleski, Philip, and Carol Zaleski. *The Fellowship: The Literary Lives of the Inklings*. New York: Farrar, Straus and Giroux, 2015.

Contributors

Adam L. Brackin
http://www.AdamBrackin.com

Adam L. Brackin, Ph.D — Doc to his friends — is an independent media consultant, new-media apologist, writer, and sometimes professor. His teaching and research interests include: Social Media, Transmedia, and ARG; all forms of non-linear and interactive narrative; story mechanics models, and video game studies and design.

Annie Crawford

Annie Crawford lives in Austin, Texas with her husband and three teenage daughters. She currently homeschools, teaches humanities courses, and serves on the Faith & Culture team at Christ Church Anglican while working to complete a Masters of Apologetics at Houston Baptist University.

Virginia de la Lastra

Virginia de la Lastra is an MD from Chile with a specialty in clinical microbiology. She works at Universidad de los Andes medical school, Hospital Dipreca, Teen Star program, and at the Reproductive Health Research Institute (RHRI). In 2016, she earned a Master's degree in Apologetics from Houston Baptist University. During her studies there, she discovered a love for drawing and has been doing it ever since. Now, she illustrates for the *American Chesterton Society*, *An Unexpected Journal*, *Sociedad de Chesterton Chile*, *Teen Star* program, *RHRI*, and of course, for her medical students, nieces, nephews and little neighbors.

Brenton Dickieson
http://www.aPilgrimInNarnia.com

Brenton Dickieson is writing a PhD thesis on the spiritual theology of C.S. Lewis at the University of Chester. He teaches at Signum University and The King's College, and writes the popular faith, fiction, and fantasy blog, www.aPilgrimInNarnia.com.

Ryan Grube

Ryan Grube earned his M.A. in Apologetics from HBU, where he studied under Drs. Ordway and Ward, among others. The experience led him to undertake a multi-year, cross-disciplinary study of semiotics and formal causality, the lessons of which he hopes to share soon in published form.

Malcolm Guite
https://malcolmguite.wordpress.com/blog/

Malcolm Guite is a poet and priest, working as Chaplain of Girton College, Cambridge. He also teaches for the Divinity Faculty and for the Cambridge Theological Federation, and lectures widely in England and North America on Theology and Literature. He is the author of *What do Christians Believe?* Granta (2006); *Faith Hope and Poetry* (Ashgate 2010, paperback 2012); *Sounding the Seasons: Seventy Sonnets for the Christian Year* (Canterbury 2012); *The Singing Bowl: Collected Poems* (Canterbury 2013); *The Word in the Wilderness* (Canterbury 2014); *Waiting on the Word* (Canterbury Press 2015); and *Parable and Paradox* (Canterbury Press 2016). He contributed the Chapter on Lewis as a poet to the *Cambridge Companion to C.S. Lewis* (CUP 2010).

Marshall Arthur Liszt

Marshall Arthur Liszt is a multimedia artist, freelance photographer, and longtime admirer of *Planet Narnia* whose most recent interests include liminality, environmental hiddenness, and numinous suggestion. He frequently alternates between academic and aesthetic pursuits, especially where they intersect with theology.

Louis Markos
http://www.LouMarkos.com

Louis Markos, Professor in English and Scholar in Residence at Houston Baptist University, holds the Robert H. Ray Chair in Humanities; his 18 books include *On The Shoulders of Hobbits* and *Lewis Agonistes*.

Jason Monroe
https://medium.com/@WellAtW0r1dsEnd

Jason holds a B.A. from York College in York, NE, where he studied English and Psychology. He also recently completed his M.A. in Christian Apologetics from Houston Baptist University. He grew up in Pierre, SD and currently lives in Spearfish, SD. His primary research and writing interests are Inklings studies, philosophy of science, and Catholic theology. He volunteers at his local parish as a cantor, drummer, and RCIA teacher, and he likes to hike and snowboard in the beautiful Black Hills.

Holly Ordway
http://www.hollyordway.com

Holly Ordway is Professor of English and a faculty member in the M.A. in Apologetics at Houston Baptist University; she holds a PhD in English from the University of Massachusetts Amherst. Her most recent book is *Apologetics and the Christian Imagination: An Integrated Approach to Defending the Faith* (Emmaus Road, 2017); she has contributed chapters to volumes such as *C.S. Lewis at Poets' Corner*; *C.S. Lewis's List*; *Women and C.S. Lewis*; and *The Inklings and King Arthur*. She is also a Subject Editor for the Journal of Inklings Studies and a published poet. Her academic work focuses on imaginative and literary apologetics, and on the writings of C.S. Lewis and J.R.R. Tolkien. Her current book project is *Tolkien's Modern Sources: Middle-earth Beyond the Middle Ages* (forthcoming from Kent State University Press, 2019).

Jahdiel Perez

Jahdiel Perez is a D.Phil (Ph.D) Candidate of Theology and Literature at the University of Oxford. He is President of the Oxford C.S. Lewis Society and also a Doctoral Fellow at the Oxford Centre for Christian Apologetics. Under the supervision of Alister McGrath and Michael Ward, Jahdiel's doctoral work seeks to develop a theology of laughter from the writings of C.S. Lewis. Prior to Oxford, Jahdiel was preaching and teaching at his home church in Boston, Massachusetts, while earning an M.Div from Harvard University. He lives in St. Stephen's House, Oxford, with his wife Ariel.

Josiah Peterson

Josiah Peterson is debate coach and instructor of rhetoric at the King's College and is enrolled in HBU's MAA program in Cultural Apologetics. He lives in New York with his wife Rachelle and daughter Hosanna. His primary scholarly interest is in the work of C.S. Lewis.

John Mark Reynolds

Dr. John Mark Reynolds is the President of the Saint Constantine School, a kindergarten through college program describe by the national media as one of the most radical ideas in college education.

He's is a senior fellow in the humanities at The Kings College and a Fellow of the Center For Science and Culture at The Discovery Institute. He is the former provost of Houston Baptist University. He was the founder and director of the Torrey Honors Institute, the Socratic, great books-centered honors program at Biola University. He received his Ph.D. in Philosophy from the University of Rochester, where he wrote his dissertation analyzing cosmology and psychology in Plato's Timaeus. Dr. Reynolds is the author of numerous books, including When Athens Met Jerusalem: an Introduction to Classical and Christian Thought and is the editor of The Great Books Reader. He is a frequent blogger and lecturer on a wide range of topics including ancient philosophy, classical and home education, politics, faith, and virtue.

John Mark attends St. Paul Orthodox Church in Katy, Texas with his parents, brother, wife, and children. An avid technophile, the lights, speakers, and computers in his house can all be controlled by his phone, to both cool and disastrous effect. He loves Disneyland, Star Trek, and the Green Bay Packers. John Mark and his wife Hope have four homeschool-graduate children: L.D., Mary Kate, Ian and Jane.

Lancia E. Smith
https://thecultivatingproject.com

Lancia E. Smith is an author, photographer, teacher, and business owner based in Colorado. She is editor-in-chief of the online quarterly magazine *Cultivating the Good, True, & Beautiful*, and is founder of *The Cultivating Project*, a discipling initiative for Christians engaged in the arts.

Donald T. Williams
http://www.donaldtwilliams.com

Donald T. Williams, PhD, is a border dweller, permanently camped out on the borders between theology and literatyre, serious scholarship and pastoral ministry, Narnia and Middle Earth. He serves as R. A. Forrest Scholar at Toccoa Falls College and is the author of *Deeper Magic: The Theology behind the Writings of C. S. Lewis* (Baltimore: Square Halo Press, 2016).

Michael Ward
http://www.michaelward.net

Michael Ward is Senior Research Fellow at Blackfriars Hall, University of Oxford, and Professor of Apologetics at Houston Baptist University, Texas. Professor Ward is the author of *Planet Narnia: The Seven Heavens in the Imagination of C.S. Lewis* (Oxford University Press), co-editor of *The Cambridge Companion to C.S. Lewis* (Cambridge University Press) and presenter of the BBC television documentary, *The Narnia Code*. On the fiftieth anniversary of Lewis's death (22 November 2013), Dr. Ward had the privilege of unveiling a permanent national memorial to him in Poets' Corner, Westminster Abbey, London. He is the co-editor of a book of essays about this commemoration, entitled *C.S. Lewis at Poets' Corner*

(Wipf & Stock). He studied English at Oxford, Theology at Cambridge, and has a PhD in Divinity from the University of St Andrews and an honorary doctorate in letters from Hillsdale College, Michigan. For three years in the 1990s he worked as resident warden of The Kilns, Lewis's Oxford home. He has been described by The Times Literary Supplement as 'the foremost living Lewis scholar'. Michael's chief claim to fame, however, is that he handed a pair of X-ray spectacles to 007 in the James Bond movie *The World Is Not Enough*.

Kyoko Yuasa
http://www.facebook.com/kyoko.yuasa

Kyoko Yuasa is a lecturer of English Literature at Fuji Women's University, Japan. She is the author of "C.S. Lewis and Christian Postmodernism: Jewish Laughter Reversed" in *Inklings Forever* (2017), *C. S. Lewis and Christian Postmodernism: Word, Image and Beyond* (2016), and Japanese translator of Bruce L. Edwards's *A Rhetoric of Reading: C.S. Lewis's Defense of Western Literacy* (2007).

About AUJ

J. R. R. Tolkien and C. S. Lewis, both members of The Inklings writers group, are well-known for their fiction embedded with Christian themes. These fantasy writers, who were also philosophers and teachers, understood the important role imagination plays in both exercising and expanding the faculties of the mind as well as the development of faith.

Beyond the parables of Jesus, their works are the gold standard for imaginative apologetics. The title, *An Unexpected Journal*, is a nod to the work to which Tolkien devoted much of his life, *The Lord of the Rings*.

An Unexpected Journal is the endeavor of a jovial band of apologists trained at Houston Baptist University. What began as simply a Facebook post on 1 November, 2017, wishing for an outlet for imaginative apologetics quickly organized into a very real and very exciting quarterly publication. AUJ seeks to demonstrate the truth of Christianity through both reason and the imagination to engage the culture from a Christian worldview.

For subscription information, news of upcoming events, or speaking requests, please send an email to anunexpectedjournal@gmail.com. Be sure to join us online:

> anunexpectedjournal.com/
> facebook.com/anunexpectedjournal/
> twitter.com/anujournal
> instagram.com/anujournal/
> pinterest.com/anunexpectedjournal/

From A Fellow Traveller

Jack Tollers

If you aren't a Christian and have somehow gotten to the point where you are reading this, then I must warn you about the pebble in your shoe. For that is what it is like to be around Christians who discuss things together, whether or not they are "Christian kinds of things" that are discussed: At a certain point you will notice something about their point of view, something in their underlying assumptions, and to be honest when you do it will become quite annoying.

That is the pebble I was referring to.

But it gets worse.

Maybe it is not your fault that you happen to be reading this, and you've done a pretty good job milling about life without bumping into too much of this sort of Christian stuff. It could be the case that you haven't really made a conscious effort to avoid Christianity, but chances are (if you are reading this) that is going to change. Somewhere along the line, perhaps even in the course of reading this journal, even, a pebble has worked its way into your shoe, and eventually the pebble will have to be dealt with.

May I suggest to you that the pebble does not exist solely to annoy you. It annoys so that you stop and deal with it. This will lead to thinking about your shoe. Then about how much further up the trail you'd be if it weren't for that blasted pebble, and eventually you'll be having thoughts about the trail itself and the path you're on in life … and so on.

One particular Christian, or a single thought expressed by a Christian, or perhaps just the peculiar quality you meet in places and things of Christian origin — these are pebbles whose ultimate function is to put you in mind of something beyond or behind themselves. (I say some*thing* because I'm trying to be non-partisan, but really I mean some*one*.) Eventually, the thought of things Christian changes to an awareness of the Christ person after whom all Christians are named.

When this moment comes, avoid mistaking Jesus for another pebble in your shoe. (If you do, it won't be long before another pebble gets in there and starts the whole thing off again. It took me years to figure that out.) Instead, consider the possibility that he is more like the path than the pebble. He said as much himself when he told Thomas, "I am the way, the truth and the life. No man comes to the Father except by me."

The truth aspect of Jesus' claim is, of course, exclusive. But there is more to his self disclosure. The other terms, "the way" and "the life" point us beyond a mere static assertion of fact or a single point of view toward a dynamic process of relational involvement. The pursuit of truth itself cannot help but lead to knowing Jesus (if he is indeed truth incarnate as Christians claim).

Thus, just as travelers come to know a country by living in it and exploring it, so people will grow in their knowledge of Truth as they make their way through life, the path itself bringing us in proximity to Jesus. Such a journey, so conceived, is bound to take a person through some interesting experiences, and to unexpected places. Once the pebble is out of the shoe.

> All the way to heaven is heaven for he said, "I am the way"
> — St. Catherine of Sienna

> "And ye shall seek me, and find me,
> when ye shall search for me with all your heart."
> — Jeremiah 29:13

Made in the USA
Lexington, KY
12 December 2019